The Child Development Associate®
National Credentialing Program
and
CDA® Competency Standards

COUNCIL
— *for* —
PROFESSIONAL
RECOGNITION

Council for Professional Recognition

2460 16th Street, NW, Washington, DC 20009-3547

800-424-4310

Visit the Council's Website at **www.cdacouncil.org**.

Preschool Edition

Eleventh Printing, Printed and bound in the United States of America

April 2019

ISBN: 978-0-9889650-0-3

Table of Contents

Part 1

Part 2

The Child Development Associate® Competency Standards 37

Part 3

Introduction

Dr. Calvin E. Moore, Jr.
Deputy Director, Office of Child Care
U.S. Department of Health and Human Services
Earned his CDA in 1992

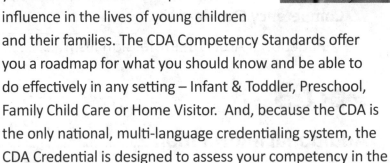

Dear Colleagues:

We welcome you as you begin your journey to earn your Child Development Associate® (CDA) Credential™!

The CDA® is the "best first step" you can take to become a powerful influence in the lives of young children and their families. The CDA Competency Standards offer you a roadmap for what you should know and be able to do effectively in any setting – Infant & Toddler, Preschool, Family Child Care or Home Visitor. And, because the CDA is the only national, multi-language credentialing system, the CDA Credential is designed to assess your competency in the language of your daily work.

Since 1971, the CDA National Credentialing Program has been the only comprehensive system of its kind in our country. We are proud that the CDA continues to be the nation's premier credential for early educators. If you move to another state or community, you can be confident knowing that the CDA is the only portable, transferable, valid, competency-based, national credential recognized

MaryEllen Fritz
President and CEO, Family Resource Center
Earned her CDA in 2002

Cristy Lopez
Teacher
Earned her CDA in 2012

Sabrena Smith
Director of Training Programs
Earned her CDA in 1990

Aisha Batty
Family Child Care Provider
Earned her CDA in 1993

Betsy Thompson
The first high school student to be awarded a CDA (2012)

Brenda Acero
The 300,000ᵗʰ CDA awarded (2012)

in all 50 states, territories, the District of Columbia, community colleges and the United States military. The CDA is the only credit-bearing national credential that articulates to Associate degrees in most community college systems across the nation. When you earn your CDA, you join a community of over 425,000 early educators!

All of us as at the Council consider our relationship with you to be a sacred trust. We are deeply committed to supporting your professional growth and progress. We look forward to awarding your CDA Credential — a powerful symbol of your accomplishments. We are with you as you take the journey to make an even more powerful difference in the lives of young children!

Sincerely,

Valora Washington

Valora Washington, PhD
CEO
Council for Professional Recognition

Michelle Salcedo
Chief Academic Officer
Earned her CDA in 1994

Jacqueline Whiting
Teacher
Earned her CDA in 1991

Tracy Ehlert
Teacher
Earned her CDA in 2010

Overview

The Child Development Associate® (CDA) Credential™ is the most widely recognized credential in early childhood education (ECE) and is a key stepping stone on the path of career advancement in ECE. The CDA® Credential is based on a core set of Competency Standards, which guide early care and learning professionals as they work toward becoming qualified teachers of young children. These professionals have the knowledge of how to put the CDA Competency Standards into practice and the understanding of how the Standards help children move with success from one developmental stage to another.

The Child Development Associate® (CDA) Credential™ is the "best first step" because:

The CDA® National Credentialing Program is based on the knowledge of the nation's leading scholars in early care and learning. Utilizing multiple sources of evidence, the Program is the only comprehensive system of its kind that recognizes the essential competencies needed by entry-level and all early childhood professionals. The CDA credentialing process is now a powerful, cohesive professional development experience, infused with meaningful activities that facilitate the reflective practice of working professionals.

The CDA Credential is awarded to early care and learning professionals who work in a variety of settings:

- **Infant/Toddler**
- **Preschool**
- **Family Child Care**
- **Home Visitors**

Candidates may also apply for Language Specializations:

- **Bilingual Specialization** (for Candidates working in bilingual programs)
- **Monolingual Specialization** (for Candidates working in programs in which a language other than English is spoken) Note: If the language of the Specialization is other than Spanish, the Candidate must contact the Council in order to make special arrangements.

The **Child Development Associate® (CDA) National Credentialing Program** was established in 1971. The purpose of the program is to enhance the quality of early care and learning by defining, evaluating and recognizing the competence of early care and learning professionals across the country. More than 425,000 child care providers have earned the CDA® Credential since 1975, in all 50 states as well as the U.S. territories of Guam, the Virgin Islands and the Commonwealth of Puerto Rico.

The CDA assessment and credentialing of early care and learning professionals has been administered by the Council for Professional Recognition since 1985.

Mission of the Council

The Council for Professional Recognition promotes improved performance and recognition of professionals in the early childhood education of children aged birth to 5 years old.

Vision of the Council

The Council works to ensure that all early care and learning professionals meet the developmental, emotional and educational needs of our nation's (the world's) youngest children.

Identity of the Council

The Council has, for decades, viewed itself as an "assessment" organization whose purpose is to assess the competency of early care and learning professionals and award the CDA® Credential to all Candidates who meet eligibility requirements and show evidence of meeting the Council's Competency Standards.

Upon the arrival of the Council's current CEO, Valora Washington, in January, 2011, the Council now views itself as having an expanded identity: The Council remains an assessment organization but is also a professional development (PD) organization in which the CDA is the first best step along the PD path. This paradigm shift opens new opportunities for the Council to increase the ways the Mission is met and expand the Vision to include more ways to be of support to young children and the professionals who serve them.

Settings for CDA® Assessments

Candidates applying for the CDA Credential must be observed working in a "setting" that meets the following criteria: (NOTE: Candidates may be employed or work on a volunteer basis in the child care setting.)

CENTER BASED SETTING

Preschool Center Based setting is a state-approved child development center where a Candidate can be observed working with a group of at least eight children, all of whom are ages 3 to 5 years. In addition, a center-based program must have: (1) at least 10 children enrolled in the program (not necessarily in the Candidate's group); and (2) at least two caregivers working with the children on a regular basis.

Infant-Toddler Center Based setting is a state-approved child development center where a Candidate can be observed working with a group of at least three children, all of whom are aged birth through 36 months. A Candidate may work/be observed with all sub-groups or with one or two sub-groups*). In addition, a center-based program must have: (1) at least 10 children enrolled in the program (not necessarily in the Candidate's group); and (2) at least two caregivers working with the children on a regular basis.

FAMILY CHILD CARE SETTING

A **Family Child Care** setting is a family child care home where a Candidate can be observed working with at least two children 5 years old or younger who are not related to the Candidate by blood or marriage. The setting must meet at least the minimum level of applicable state and/or local regulations. Family Child Care settings are also eligible in localities where there is no regulation of family child care.

Important note: In states where there are licensed 'group homes,' these meet the CDA requirements for a family child care setting. However, in group homes where 10 or more children are enrolled and at least 2 caregivers work with the children on a regular basis, Candidates may apply for the center-base credential.

HOME VISITOR SETTING

A **Home Visitor** setting is an established program of Home visits (to families with children 5 years old or younger) that supports parents in meeting the needs of their young children, and where Candidates can be observed conducting home visits. In this setting, regular home visits are the primary methods of program delivery.

~ BILINGUAL SETTING
(Required for Candidates who apply for Bilingual Specialization)

A **Bilingual** setting is a child development program that has specific goals for achieving bilingual development in children; where two languages are consistently used in daily experiences and activities; and where parents are helped to understand the goals and support children's dual language learning.

SPECIAL EDUCATION SETTING

A **"Special Education"** child development setting – one designed to serve children with moderate to severe special needs – does qualify as an eligible setting for CDA assessment. The CDA Competency Standards address the skills that early childhood educators need for this population of children. The program must meet the other criteria described above for a Preschool, Infant/Toddler, or Family Child Care setting. The chronological ages of the children with special needs also must match the age groups specified for each setting.

NOTE: Drop in programs and before and after school programs are not eligible settings where a Candidate can prove his or her competence around the Competency Standards including all Functional Areas.

 Indicates a required example for Candidates seeking Bilingual Specialization

Professional Portfolio

Observation

Part 1

Earning the Child Development Associate® (CDA) Credential™

1. Prepare for the CDA Credentialing Process
2. Apply for the CDA Credentialing Process
3. Demonstrate Your Competence
4. Earn Your Credential
5. Renew Your Credential

CDA Exam

Reflective Dialogue

Earning the Child Development Associate® (CDA) Credential™

In order to earn and maintain the Child Development Associate® (CDA) Credential™, Candidates must follow the following sequence of steps:

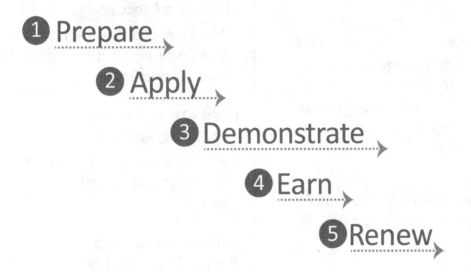

1. **Prepare**
2. **Apply**
3. **Demonstrate**
4. **Earn**
5. **Renew**

On the following pages, each of the steps is discussed in detail. You are encouraged to read through the process in its entirety in order to gain a sense of the full credentialing process and its requirements. Once you choose to begin your credentialing process, you may use the Candidate Checklist, found on the inside cover of this book, to track each of your accomplishments as you make your way toward earning the CDA.

Prepare for the CDA® Credentialing Process: Candidate Eligibility Requirements

Any Time Before You Apply

High School Education

You must have a valid high school diploma to apply for the Child Development Associate® (CDA) Credential™. A GED or enrollment as a junior or senior in a high school career/ technical program in early childhood education are also acceptable.

Literacy Skills

Be able to speak, read and write well enough, in the language required at work, to fulfill the responsibilities of a CDA®.

Setting

You must identify a state-approved child development center where you, the Candidate,

1 Prepare

Any Time Before You Apply
- High School Education
- Professional Education -- 120 clock hours, including 10 hours in each of the 8 CDA Subject Areas

Within Three Years of Submitting Application
- Work Experience --- 480 hours of experience working with children ages 3-5

Within Six Months of Submitting Application
- Family Questionnaires
- Professional Portfolio

can be observed working as **lead teacher** with a group of **at least eight children**, all of whom are ages 3 to 5 years. In addition, a center-based program must have: 1) at least 10 children enrolled in the program (not necessarily in the Candidate's group); and (2) at least two caregivers working with the children on a regular basis.

Professional Education

You must complete 120 clock hours of professional early childhood education, covering the growth and development of children ages 3 to 5 years, with no fewer than 10 hours in each of the eight CDA® Subject Areas:

The 8 CDA® Subject Areas

CDA® Subject Area 1. Planning a safe and healthy learning environment

> Examples: Safety, first aid, health, nutrition, space planning, materials and equipment, play

CDA® Subject Area 2. Advancing children's physical and intellectual development

> Examples: Large and small muscle, language and literacy, discovery, art, music, mathematics, social studies, science, technology, and dual language learning

CDA® Subject Area 3: Supporting children's social and emotional development

Examples: Adult modeling, self-esteem, self-regulation, socialization, cultural identity, conflict resolution

CDA® Subject Area 4. Building productive relationships with families

Examples: Parent involvement, home visits, conferences, referrals, communication strategies

CDA® Subject Area 5. Managing an effective program

Examples: Planning, record keeping, reporting, community services

CDA® Subject Area 6. Maintaining a commitment to professionalism

Examples: Advocacy, ethical practices, workforce issues, professional development, goal setting, networking

CDA® Subject Area 7. Observing and recording children's behavior

Examples: Tools and strategies for objective observation and assessment of children's behavior and learning to plan curriculum and individualize teaching, developmental delays, intervention strategies, individual education plans

CDA® Subject Area 8. Understanding principles of child development and learning

Examples: Typical developmental expectations for children from birth through age 5, individual variation including children with special needs, cultural influences on development, an understanding of early brain development

In order to show proof of your professional education, you must provide transcripts, certificates or letters (originals or copies) in your *Professional Portfolio* (p. 13). This documentation should be preceded by the *Summary of My CDA® Education* cover sheet, found at the end of this book on p. 135. At your CDA Verification Visit®, the CDA Professional Development (PD) Specialist™ will review the *Summary* cover sheet and attached documentation.

Acceptable Professional Education

Education may be completed through a wide variety of training organizations, including two and four year colleges, private training organizations, vocational or technical schools, resource and referral agencies and early childhood education programs that sponsor training (such as Head Start or the U.S. Military).

You may accumulate the hours from a single training program or from a combination of programs. Each agency or organization must provide verification of your education in the form of a transcript, certificate or letter on official letterhead. The Council accepts in-service training, but does not accept training obtained at conferences or from individual consultants.

All professional education hours must be awarded by an agency or organization with expertise in early childhood teacher preparation. These hours can be for college credit or for no credit.

Within Three Years Before You Apply

Work Experience

You must have at least 480 hours of experience, within the past three years, working with children ages 3-5 in a group setting to apply for the Child Development Associate® (CDA) Credential™. Your experience may be as a paid staff or volunteer.

Within Six Months Before You Apply

Family Questionnaires

Your reflections on family perceptions about your strengths and areas for professional growth are very important in the CDA® credentialing process. Each family with a child in your care should be invited to complete a questionnaire.

A *Family Questionnaire* that is reproducible is provided for you at the end of this book on p. 137. Please tear it out and make the appropriate number of copies for distribution among your families. There is also a Spanish *Family Questionnaire* for any Spanish speaking families in your program on p. 139. Note: The *Family Questionnaire* is two-sided – both sides must be copied and distributed to families.

Before copying, fill in the blank spaces in the introduction (your name and the date by which you will need the questionnaires returned to you). Copy and distribute one to each family.

Once you have collected all of the completed questionnaires, please read the responses and reflect on the feedback you have received. Do you notice any patterns or trends among the families' responses about their perceptions of your strengths or areas for professional growth? Remember that there are no "right" or "wrong" conclusions to draw, you must decide for yourself how to best interpret the feedback you have been given. For example, you might notice that 17 out of 20 questionnaires rate you as "very capable" when it comes to promoting health and nutrition (#2). You might conclude that the families, generally, see this as one of your strengths. Similarly, you might notice that 12 out of 20 rate you as "needs improvement" in the area of helping children express themselves creatively through music, art and movement (#7). You might conclude that the families, generally, see this as an area for your continued professional growth.

Conclude the *Family Questionnaire* process by writing any Areas of Strength and/or Areas for Professional Growth you've chosen on the *Family Questionnaire Summary Sheet* found at the end of this book on p. 141. Additionally, write this information in Boxes A and B of the *CDA Verification Visit® Reflective Dialogue Worksheet,* also found at the end of the book on p. 143. This step is important because your CDA Verification Visit® will conclude with a reflective dialogue/discussion with a CDA Professional Development (PD) Specialist™ in which you will consider this feedback from your families as you set professional goals for yourself.

In addition to the Areas of Strength and/or Areas for Professional Growth you've written on the *Family Questionnaire Summary Sheet*, you must also list the total number of questionnaires distributed and collected. You are required to collect the "majority" (more than half) of the questionnaires you distribute.

Place the *Family Questionnaire Summary Sheet* and completed questionnaires behind Tab B in your Professional Portfolio. Please know that no one but you will read the feedback your families have provided. The PD Specialist will only look at the Summary sheet to verify that you have successfully completed this task.

Professional Portfolio

The *Professional Portfolio* is intended to be a reflective professional development experience for you. You are encouraged to use and add to your Portfolio as you grow throughout your career.

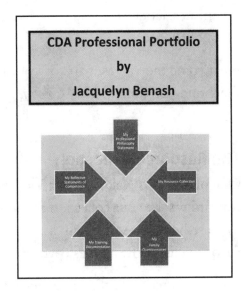

Your Professional Portfolio must include:

a) The *My CDA® Professional Portfolio* cover sheet found at the back of this book on p. 133 (this cover sheet provides greater details on the specific order of portfolio components – use it as a checklist as you build your Portfolio to ensure that your completed Portfolio contains all of the required contents)

b) The *Summary of My CDA® Education* cover sheet followed by your transcripts, certificates, letters, etc.

c) The *Family Questionnaires* cover sheet followed by your completed family questionnaires

d) Six Reflective Statements of Competence, followed by the related Resource Collection items, as outlined on the *My CDA® Professional Portfolio* cover sheet

e) Your Professional Philosophy Statement, which summarizes your professional viewpoint and may take into account new ideas you learned during the building of your Portfolio.

Preparing Your Professional Portfolio

The first step is creating the shell of your Portfolio, into which you will add many items. Your Portfolio may be arranged in any creative way you choose (for example, organized in a three-ring binder, contained inside folders in a file box or even created online). While there are no specific requirements about how it should look, it should be legible, look professional and be manageable in size and portability.

The second step will be to add your *My CDA® Professional Portfolio* cover sheet. This portfolio cover sheet will guide you in organizing the contents of your Portfolio using tabbed sections.

You will then add your *Summary of My CDA® Education* cover sheet followed by your transcripts, certificates, letters, etc. and your *Family Questionnaires* cover sheet followed by your completed family questionnaires.

Next come the biggest parts of your Portfolio preparation work – the collection of Resources and the writing of your *Reflective Competency Statements*.

The Resource Collection

One of the most valuable components of your Portfolio that you might use in your work moving forward will be your collection of early childhood resources. You may find yourself referring back to these helpful resources in the future as you continue your career. (Note: The numbering of the following list of Resources correlates to each of the Competency Standards.)

Your Resource Collection must include the following items:

RC I-1 Your valid and current certificates of completion or cards from a) any **first aid course** and b) an **infant/child (pediatric) CPR course** offered by a nationally-recognized training organization (such as American Red Cross or the American Heart Association). Online training is not acceptable.

RC I-2 A copy of **one weekly menu**. In order to complete your related Reflective Competency Statement on this topic, the menu would ideally be one that you have participated in serving to and/or designing for children. If this is not possible, or if you work in a program that does not serve meals, you may substitute a group care menu found on the internet. (More important than the source of the menu will be Reflective Competency Statement I, in which you will discuss your opinions about the menu – what you think are its strengths and/or what you might serve that you think is more appropriate and why.)

RC I-3   A sample of your **weekly plan** that includes goals for children's learning and development, brief descriptions of planned learning experiences, and also accommodations for children with special needs (whether for children you currently serve or may serve in the future). Indicate the age group(s) for which the plan is intended.

RC II   Nine **learning experiences** (activities), written in your own words, including one from each of the following curricular areas:

RC II-1 Science/Sensory

RC II-2 Language and Literacy

RC II-3 Creative Arts

RC II-4 Fine motor (please choose an indoor activity)

RC II-5 Gross motor (please choose an outdoor activity)

RC II-6 Self Concept

RC II-7 Emotional Skills/ Regulation

RC II-8 Social Skills

RC II-9 Mathematics

For example, for RC II-1, Science/Sensory, you might write about an experience entitled "Smell Jars" and for RC II-6, Self Concept, you might write about an experience entitled "Self Portraits".

For each experience, indicate the age group (3s, 4s or 5s) and list the intended goals, materials and processes/teaching strategies. For each activity, discuss why it is developmentally appropriate for that age group.

RC III   A **bibliography** that includes the titles, authors, publishers, copyright dates and short summaries of ten developmentally appropriate children's books that you have used with young children. Each book should support a different topic related to children's lives and challenges. Subjects you might consider addressing include:

• Cultural or linguistic group identity

• Gender Identity

• Children with Special Needs

• Separation/Divorce/Remarriage/Family Structures

• Phases of the cycle of life from human reproduction to death

• Other topics that reflect the children and families with whom you work

RC IV   A **Family Resources Guide** that you might choose to share with the families you serve. The Guide should include all of the helpful information you think they might need. At a minimum, you must include the following required items:

RC IV-1   The name and contact information (phone number, web site, etc.) of a local agency that provides family counseling.

RC IV-2   The name and contact information (phone number, web site, etc.) of a translation service for families whose home language is other than English as well as a service that provides American Sign Language translation.

RC IV-3   The name, contact information and brief descriptions of at least two agencies in the community that provide resources and services for children with disabilities (in most communities, the local school district provides these services).

RC IV-4   A list of three or more websites, and brief descriptions of each, that provide current information to help families understand how young children develop and learn. Include one current article for each website. Web sites must contain articles that help families understand the development and learning of 3- to 5-year-olds. At least one article must relate to child guidance.

RC V   Three samples of **record keeping forms** you use/have used. Include an accident report form, an emergency form and a completed tool/form that you have used to observe for and document a child's developmental/learning progress (*Do not include the child's name*).

RC VI-1   The name and contact information of your state's agency that is responsible for **the regulation of child care centers and family child care homes**. (Note: These regulations are available at the website of the National Resource Center for Health and Safety in Child Care: *https://childcareta.acf.hhs.gov/licensing*). Make a copy of the sections that describe the qualification requirements for personnel (teachers, directors and assistants) and group size, adult-child ratio requirements:

RC VI-2   A list of two or three **early childhood associations** (national, regional, state or local), including website addresses, describing the professional resources and membership opportunities they each offer.

RC VI-3   Summaries of the **legal requirements** in your state regarding child abuse and neglect (including contact information for the appropriate agency in your state) and Mandatory Reporting Guidelines.

The Reflective Statements of Competence

Prepare six written reflections on your own teaching practices. You must write one Reflective Statement for each of the six CDA® Competency Standards (see below for specific requirements). Many of the Statements require the use of specific Resources from your *Resource Collection*, above, as the focus of that written reflection. Each Statement should be no more than 500 words in length.

CSI **Competency Statement I** *(To establish and maintain a safe, healthy learning environment)*:

Begin your Reflective Statement about this Competency Standard with a paragraph describing how your teaching practices meet this Standard (Note: alternatively, you may also choose to write one paragraph for each Functional Area, if this makes it easier to express your thoughts more clearly).

Then write at least one paragraph on each of the following:

CS I a   Reflect on the sample menu in the *Resource Collection* (RC I-2): If you designed the menu, how does it reflect your commitment to children's nutritional needs? If you did not design it, what are its strengths and/or what would you change?

CS I b   Reflect on the room environment in which your CDA Verification Visit® Observation will occur: How does the room design reflect the way you believe young children learn best? If the room was not designed by you, what do you see as its strengths and/or what would you change?

CS I c   Reflect on the weekly plan you included in your *Resource Collection* (RC I-3). How does this plan reflect your philosophy of what young children need on a weekly basis? If the plan was not designed by you, what do you see as its strengths and/or what would you change?

CSII **Competency Statement II** (To advance physical and intellectual competence):

Begin your Reflective Statement about this Competency Standard with a paragraph describing how your teaching practices meet this Standard (Note: alternatively, you may also choose to write one paragraph for each Functional Area, if this makes it easier to express your thoughts more clearly).

Then prepare at least one paragraph on each of the following:

CS II a   Pick one of the nine learning experiences you chose for your *Resource Collection* (RC II). How does this experience reflect your philosophy of how to support young children's *physical* development?

CS II b   Pick another of the nine learning experiences you chose for your *Resource Collection* (RC II). How does this experience reflect your philosophy of how to support young children's *cognitive* development?

CS II c   Pick a third learning experience you chose for your *Resource Collection* (RC II). How does this experience reflect your philosophy of how to support young children's *creative* development?

CS II d   In an additional paragraph, describe ways to promote the communication/language development among all children, including dual language learners.

CSIII   **Competency Statement III** *(To support social and emotional development and to provide positive guidance)*:

Begin your Reflective Statement about this Competency Standard with a paragraph describing how your teaching practices meet this Standard (Note: alternatively, you may also choose to write one paragraph for each Functional Area, if this makes it easier to express your thoughts more clearly).

Then prepare at least one paragraph on each of the following:

CS III a   Describe some of the ways you support the development of children's positive self-concepts and growing social/emotional skills.

CS III b   Reflect on your philosophy of guiding young children's *positive* behaviors. How is your professional philosophy similar or different from how you were guided as a child? How do you constructively deal with young children's *challenging* behaviors?

CSIV   **Competency Statement IV** *(To establish positive and productive relationships with families)*:

Begin your Reflective Statement about this Competency Standard with a paragraph describing how your teaching practices meet this Standard.

Then prepare at least one paragraph on each of the following:

CS IV a   How do you ensure that families are kept aware of what's happening in their child's daily/weekly life in your program?

CS IV b   How do you ensure that you are aware of what's happening in each child's home life? How does that awareness direct your teaching practices?

CS IV c   Reflect on the feedback you received in the *Family Questionnaires* you collected (please see pp. 12-13). Explain how the responses surprised you, confirmed your own reflections about yourself and/or gave you a new goal for professional growth.

CSV   **Competency Statement V** *(To ensure a well-run, purposeful program that is responsive to participant needs)*:

Begin your Reflective Statement about this Competency Standard with a paragraph describing how your teaching practices meet this Standard.

CS V a   Then write at least one paragraph that describes how you used the observation tool/form you included in the Resource Collection (RC V). Why are observation and documentation important parts of program management? How do you ensure that you are accurately/objectively observing and tracking each child's developmental and learning progress?

CSVI   **Competency Statement VI** *(To maintain a commitment to professionalism)*:

Begin your Reflective Statement about this Competency Standard with a paragraph describing how your professional practices meet this Standard. Then:

CS VI a   Reflect on why you chose to become an early childhood professional.

CS VI b   Reflect on what you believe are the most important indicators of professionalism that you possess.

The Professional Philosophy Statement

The *Professional Philosophy Statement* is the final reflective task in the creation of your *Professional Portfolio.* Here you will summarize your professional beliefs and values about early childhood education after you have completed the professional development experience of designing your Portfolio by collecting resources and writing all six *Reflective Statements of Competence.* The *Professional Philosophy Statement* should be no more than two pages in length.

Identify your personal values and beliefs around teaching and learning: How do you believe young children learn? Based on this, what do you believe your role is? Beyond teaching and learning, reflect and write about what you believe are the other important aspects of your role in the lives of children and families.

Bring Your Professional Portfolio to your CDA Verification Visit®!

Once you have completed the preparation of your *Professional Portfolio*, please hold on to it until your CDA Verification Visit, at which time your PD Specialist will review it.

Note: You are required to present your Portfolio to your PD Specialist at the time of your CDA Verification Visit. Please do not send your Professional Portfolio to the Council at any time. The Council will not return any portfolios.

Apply for the CDA® Credentialing Process

Identify a CDA Preschool Professional Development (PD) Specialist™ and obtain his or her identification number.

The application requires you to identify a CDA Professional Development (PD) Specialist™ with Preschool endorsement (officially approved by the Council to conduct Preschool Assessments) who will agree to conduct your CDA Verification Visit®. Once the PD Specialist agrees, he/she will provide you with their Identification Number. You will need to include this number in your application.

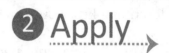

2 Apply

- Identify a CDA Professional Development Specialist™ and obtain her or his Identification Number

- Secure your director's permission for your CDA Verification Visit®

- Submit the CDA application to the Council and pay the assessment fee

The Council uses the PD Specialist Identification Number to ensure that you have chosen a PD Specialist who has been trained by the Council and is currently available to conduct CDA Verification Visits in your area. The Council will process your application only after confirming that you have identified an appropriate PD Specialist to conduct your CDA Verification Visit.

Finding a CDA PD Specialist™

There are four ways to find a PD Specialist:

- Ask someone you know who is already a PD Specialist with a Preschool endorsement.

- Ask an early childhood professional in your community to become a PD Specialist, directing them to _yourcouncil.org_ to apply for and take an online training to serve in the role.

Note: If you choose options 1 or 2, please give careful, ethical consideration to the Council's Conflicts of Interest policy on the next page.

- Go to _www.cdacouncil.org/findapds_ to use the Find-a-PD Specialist online tool, which will send a request on your behalf to a local PD Specialist.

- If none of the above methods work, you may call the Council at 800-424-4310.

CDA PD Specialist™ Eligibility Requirements

A wide range of experienced early childhood professionals may serve as PD Specialists. Please see p. 116 for the complete list of PD Specialist eligibility requirements.

CDA PD Specialist™ Conflicts of Interest

Although a particular individual may meet all of the general eligibility requirements to become a PD Specialist, you and your prospective PD Specialist must decide, together, if there are any ethical conflicts of interests related to your relationship that may disqualify her/him from serving as your PD Specialist.

No person may serve as your PD Specialist if she/he is:

1. your immediate relative (mother, father, sibling, spouse, son, daughter)

2. your current direct supervisor

3. A co-worker in same group/classroom that you work

If you are in any of these three types of relationships with this person, you may not, under any circumstances, choose this person as your PD Specialist.

However, there are many other types of relationships that will require both you and your prospective PD Specialist to consider carefully. Positions of a prospective PD Specialist that bear ethical consideration by you both are:

- Indirect supervisor

- Trainer, either indirect or direct

- Any person or representative of an organization that has financial/contractual considerations related to you or may benefit in any way from your credentialing outcome

- Your employer

- A co-employee in the same facility, not in the same group/classroom

- A peer/friend

- Any person who may have a personal or professional bias toward or against you or any group of which you are a part

- A licensing agent

The Council will not exclude any person with a relationship that may fall in one or more of the categories in the "ethical considerations" list, above, from applying, but reserves the right to enact further inquiries and end the service of a PD Specialist and/or application of a Candidate at any time should a question of conflict arise. Please note that every PD Specialist and Candidate will both be asked to sign a Statement of Ethics.

Secure your director's permission for your CDA Verification Visit®

The application requires the signature of your center/program director to confirm the following:

- The CDA Verification Visit can happen during the center/program's work hours.

- The CDA Professional Development (PD) Specialist™ will be allowed to observe you working with children in your classroom.

- During the CDA Verification Visit, you can be observed leading children's activities.

- You and your PD Specialist will be provided a quiet space if you are planning to complete the Review and/or Reflect sessions of your CDA Verification Visit on the premises of your center/program.

Complete the CDA® application

Apply online at *yourcouncil.org*. If you do not have online access, you may use the paper application found at the end of this book.

In the online or paper application, you will confirm that you have completed all preparation requirements found on pp. 10-19 of this book. You will also choose the language of your CDA® Exam (English or Spanish, regardless of the language you choose for your CDA Verification Visit®). To ensure a speedy and smooth credentialing process, follow the directions closely and do not skip any portion of the application.

Please be sure to carefully complete each section of your application and to sign it at the end. Failure to complete any part of the application will result in delayed processing times as the Council must then return the application to you for correction. The Council cannot guarantee a timely credentialing decision if you do not properly complete your application. If you have missing

Apply Online!

The *YourCouncil* online application, found at *yourcouncil.org* is simple and easy to use. Applying for your credential online will significantly speed up your credentialing process. Using the *YourCouncil®* online application you can:

- Save your work and continue later

- Check your status anytime

- Pay the assessment fee online

- Communicate quickly with the Council

- Get automatic updates as to where you are in the credentialing process

information in your application, the Council will inform you and give you 60 days to correct it, after which time you will forfeit your assessment fee and will need to start the credentialing process over, including the payment of a new assessment fee.

Note: If you change your name and/or address any time after you submit your CDA application, please inform the Council's customer support line 1-800-424-4310, as soon as possible so that, if you are awarded the CDA credential, you can be certain that the Council prints your name accordingly.

The current assessment fee can be found on the application and on the Council's website, _www.cdacouncil.org_.

You must submit the complete assessment fee with your application. You may pay the assessment fee via credit card, check, money order or agency scholarship. If you pay with an agency scholarship, you will need to provide documentation of this scholarship through a payment authorization letter from the agency.

Email Will Speed up Your CDA Credentialing Process!

Don't yet have an email address? Don't spend another day out of the loop! You can get a free email account through many different online providers including gmail.com, yahoo.com and hotmail.com.

If the Council has your correct email address, you will receive:

- The *Ready to Schedule* notice, once your CDA application is reviewed and approved by the Council

- Reminders to schedule your CDA Verification Visit® and CDA Exam before the six-month deadline

- A renewal reminder before your CDA Credential expires

- Updates about any important changes to the CDA process and Council services

- The CounciLINK monthly e-newsletter, filled with valuable resources and news for the national CDA Community

---

Demonstrate Your Competence

After the Council has processed your application and payment, you will receive a *Ready to Schedule* notification. This will be sent via email if you provided an email address or by mail if you did not.

Note: If you provided an email address, the email notification will come from the following email address: *info@yourcouncil.org*. Please add this address to your email address book to ensure that your notification is delivered to your Inbox, rather than your Junk Mail/Spam Folder.

Once the Council has approved your application and processed your payment, you must schedule and complete the following:

- Your CDA Verification Visit®
- Your CDA Exam

You may complete your CDA Verification Visit® and take the CDA® Exam as quickly as you would like and in whichever order works best for you. However, **you must complete both within six months** from the date of your *Ready to Schedule* notice. If you do not complete your CDA Exam and CDA Verification Visit within six months, you will forfeit your application fee and your Candidate record will be closed. If this happens, you will need to begin the CDA credentialing process from the beginning and pay a new assessment fee.

The CDA Verification Visit®

Scheduling Your CDA Verification Visit®

When you receive your *Ready to Schedule* notification, your CDA Professional Development (PD) Specialist™ will also receive an email notifying her/him that you are ready to schedule your CDA Verification Visit. While your PD Specialist will be required to make contact with you within five business days, the Council encourages you to take ownership of your credentialing process by reaching out to her/him first. Together you will then determine the date and time for your CDA Verification Visit. Please be sure to confirm these arrangements with your Director. Once confirmed, you may find it helpful to write the date and time in the appropriate space on the Candidate Checklist, found on the inside front cover of this book.

You must bring the following items to your CDA Verification Visit:

- Your original, complete Professional Portfolio, including all of the required contents listed on the *Professional Portfolio* cover sheet (found at the end of this book):

- Transcripts, certificates, documentation of your professional education
- *Family Questionnaires*
- *Resource Collection*
- *Six Reflective Statements of Competence*
- *Professional Philosophy Statement*

- This *Competency Standards* book, including:

  - The blank *Comprehensive Scoring Instrument* your PD Specialist will use (found at the end of this book)
  - The *Reflective Dialogue* worksheet (also found at the end of this book), with the "Areas of Strength" and "Areas for Professional Growth" boxes from the *Family Questionnaires* completed

Rescheduling Your CDA Verification Visit®

Any time prior to the CDA Verification Visit, you and/or your CDA Professional Development (PD) Specialist™ may reschedule the CDA Verification Visit. If you cannot agree on a new date and time for the CDA Verification Visit, you may find a different PD Specialist without penalty. You must contact the Council and give the Council the ID number of the new PD Specialist prior to the rescheduled CDA Verification Visit.

If your PD Specialist arrives for your CDA Verification Visit and you are not there within 15 minutes of the scheduled time, she/he will record your CDA Verification Visit as a "no-show". If this happens, you cannot earn a CDA® Credential until you reschedule your Visit with that PD Specialist or find another PD Specialist to complete your CDA Verification Visit within your initial six-month window. In order to do this you must first contact the Council at 800-424-4310 for authorization. At that time, you will be required to pay an additional $125 fee (which covers the PD Specialist honorarium from the first Visit as well as Council processing costs).

Meeting All Requirements

If your CDA Professional Development (PD) Specialist™ determines that you did not meet either of the requirements of a) your professional education documentation or b) your First Aid/Pediatric CPR, she/he will inform you at the completion of your CDA Verification Visit. Shortly thereafter, you will receive a postcard from the Council notifying you of the required procedures for correcting these errors within six months of your *Ready to Schedule* notice. If you do not correct these requirements within this time frame, you will forfeit your assessment fee and will need to start the credentialing process over, including the payment of a new assessment fee.

Your CDA Verification Visit®

At your CDA Verification Visit, your CDA Professional Development (PD) Specialist™ will utilize the R.O.R Model® to verify key aspects of your professional competency. "R.O.R." stands for Review-Observe-Reflect®. During the CDA Verification Visit, the Specialist will:

Review *the contents of your Professional Portfolio.* You will need to ensure that your PD Specialist has a quiet space, with a tabletop surface, where she/he can review your materials for sixty minutes.

Observe *you working with children.* The PD Specialist will sit silently observing you leading program activities with children for two hours. You must work with your PD Specialist in advance to ensure that you schedule the observation for a two-hour window in which the children will be awake and that you will be working with them the entire time.

Reflect *with you.* After the Review and Observe sessions, you will meet with your PD Specialist for a reflective dialogue in which you will discuss your areas of strength or growth, for the purpose of setting professional goals. This reflective dialogue, though required, has no influence on whether or not you earn the CDA® Credential. It is provided to support your professional growth and will follow a specific, set agenda (please see pp 116-118). Any goals you may set will be yours, privately, and will not be sent to the Council. However, the Council encourages you to share your goals with a trusted peer, mentor or even your supervisor. Research shows that professionals are more likely to meet the goals they have set for themselves when they have another person to offer support and hold them accountable.

During the Visit, the Specialist will use the Comprehensive Scoring Instrument at the back of this book to determine

In coordination with your PD Specialist, you have the flexibility to schedule the one hour **Review** of materials any time before or after the two hour **Observation**.

The **Reflect** session must occur last – either immediately following the Observation and Review Sessions, later in the day (for example, during Nap Time) or on another day that week (for example, on Saturday).

However, all three Sessions must be completed *within 7 consecutive days*.

Recommended Scores for each of the 51 Items in each of the thirteen Functional Areas found on pp. 42-106 in this book, using a combination of evidence found in your Professional Portfolio and through her/his observation of you working with children.

The PD Specialist will then submit Recommended Scores to the Council online within 48 hours of your CDA Verification Visit. These scores, along with the CDA Exam score, will be combined by the Council into a final Cumulative Score which will determine your credentialing decision.

The CDA® Exam

After you receive your *Ready to Schedule* notice (which will include your Candidate ID number), you may proceed to schedule your CDA Exam. You will take the computer-based exam at a local Pearson Vue testing center. Note: There is no additional fee to take your CDA Exam.

Scheduling Your CDA® Exam

Scheduling your exam is very simple. You must contact Pearson VUE directly, via website or phone. Note: the Council is not able to schedule the CDA Exam for you.

Scheduling with Pearson Vue Online:

1. Go to *www.pearsonvue.com/cdaexam*

2. Click on the *Schedule an Exam* button on the right side of your screen

3. Click on the *Create a Web Account* link

4. Enter the Candidate ID number which you received with your *Ready to Schedule* notice from the Council (Note: You will not able to proceed without providing this number therefore you cannot schedule your CDA® Exam until you have received your *Ready to Schedule* notice)

5. Verify that all of your personal information is correct (Note: if any of your information is incorrect, please contact the Council immediately at 800-424-4310)

6. Set up your username and password, writing them down on your Candidate Checklist, found on the inside front cover of this book

7. Once you have created your Pearson Vue Web Account, you may return to *www.pearsonvue.com/cdaexam* at any time to find a testing center nearest to you based on your zip code, schedule, cancel or reschedule your CDA Exam.

> **If you create your Pearson Vue account online…**
>
> …you will be able to find the test center closest to you, look at its calendar and choose a convenient day and time for your exam. You will be able to access your account any time to get directions to the test center and to cancel or reschedule your exam.

Scheduling with Pearson Vue over the Phone:

1. Call 866-507-5627 (8:00 a.m. to 8:00 p.m. EST M-F)

2. Tell the operator your Candidate ID number or your name and that you wish to schedule the CDA® Exam.

3. Verify that all of your personal information is correct (Note: if any of your information is incorrect, please contact the Council immediately at 800-424-4310)

4. Tell the operator where and when you wish to take the CDA Exam. The operator will assist you in finding the closest exam location.

Note: Military Candidates who wish to schedule their exam at their base should do so at *www.pearsonvue.com/military*.

After you schedule your CDA Exam, you will receive a *Confirmation Note* from Pearson Vue with the location and date you chose for your CDA Exam. The confirmation will also include the address, phone number and directions to the test center you chose. Write down the address and phone number on your Candidate Checklist, found on the inside front cover of this book.

> ### Set Yourself Up for Success!
>
> Choose an exam location and date that are most convenient for you. Before you choose the test center, make sure to investigate its location, accessibility and availability of parking (review the information presented on the website or ask Pearson Vue when calling). Calculate the amount of time you will need to get to the center and choose your appointment time accordingly.
>
> You must arrive at the test center at least 15 minutes before your appointment time. Estimate how much time it will take you to get to the center. If you arrive late, you may not be able to take the exam.

Rescheduling Your CDA® Exam

If you need to reschedule the CDA Exam, you must first cancel your current appointment before you can schedule another appointment. Pearson Vue will charge you a $15 cancellation fee each time you cancel the scheduled CDA Exam. You may only use a credit card or debit card to pay the cancellation fee. You may cancel and reschedule your exam appointment via your Pearson Vue online account or you may call Pearson Vue at 1-866-507-5627 (8:00 a.m. to 8:00 p.m. EST M-F).

You will not be allowed to cancel within 24 hours of your scheduled exam. If you miss your scheduled exam, Pearson VUE will require an additional $65 for a second exam. In order to do this you must first contact the Council at 800-424-4310 for authorization.

If severe weather or a natural disaster makes the test center inaccessible or unsafe, the examination will be delayed or canceled without penalty to you. Call Pearson Vue at 1-866-507-5627 or call the test center directly for details on delays and cancellations during severe weather.

Preparing for Your CDA® Exam

The CDA Exam covers practical examples of early childhood best practices; the material found in the CDA Competency Standards and Functional Areas. Your 120 hours of professional education and 480 hours working with young children should prepare you for the Exam. For a refresher, you might review the Competency Standards section of this book and "CDA Exam Questions" on pp. 121-122.

Taking Your CDA® Exam

You will be able to take the CDA Exam only one time during your credentialing process.

Before the Exam Begins

The Exam will be presented to you in English or Spanish, depending on the choice you indicated on your CDA application. Before the exam begins, the computer program will give you 15 minutes to review instructions, to agree to the required Nondisclosure Agreement, and to practice clicking with your mouse by answering three practice questions.

You will then have one hour and 45 minutes to complete the exam, however most Candidates find that they are able to complete the Exam in an hour or less. Note: the computer program will remind you when you have 30 minutes and 10 minutes left.

Rules and Procedures at Pearson Vue Testing Centers

- A valid photo ID will be required to take your Exam. The photo ID must include your signature. The photo ID you present at the test center must match the name you included on your CDA application. Note: If you got married or divorced since the time you completed your application to the Council, you must bring a marriage certificate or divorce decree with you to the test center.

- You will be asked to sign a required agreement to follow Pearson Vue's test-taking rules.

- Before entering the testing room, the Pearson Vue proctor will ask you to leave all of your personal belongings outside the testing room, in a locker or your car.

- Your friends or relatives will not be able to wait for you in the waiting area.

- You may get up to use the bathroom during the exam, but your timer will continue to run.

- Always raise your hand if you need assistance of any kind. Do not hesitate to ask for help if you are experiencing technical problems.

- There will be other test takers in the room with you. Always be respectful and try not to disrupt others.

The CDA® Exam has 65 multiple choice questions including five that have a photo and a brief classroom scenario. The questions will be presented to you one at a time. You may freely move between questions, choosing and changing your answers, as long as time permits.

 *The CDA® Exam has been designed to be easy-to-take for those new to computers. You will only need to know how to point and single click a mouse in order to complete the Exam.*

Try to answer all the questions, even if you have to guess. Questions that are left unanswered will be marked as wrong. If you are not sure of the best answer, you may "flag" the question to come back to later. After you have viewed all of the 65 questions, you will be shown a "Review" screen. The Review screen is a summary of all of your answers including the questions you did not answer (incomplete) and which questions you flagged to come back to later. If time permits, you may go back and answer the questions you flagged or did not answer. When you are ready, click "End the Review". Once you do this, you will no longer be able to go back to review or change your answers.

> ## Exam Tutorial
>
> The Council has created a tutorial to help you learn how to use the various functions of the CDA Exam screens.
>
> You will find the tutorial by visiting *www.cdacouncil.org/CDAexam/tutorial*.

When you are done, you must click the "End Exam" button before leaving the testing room. Your exam answers will then be immediately transmitted to the Council for Professional Recognition.

Your CDA Exam scores, along with your CDA Verification Visit® Recommended Scores, submitted by your CDA Professional Development (PD) Specialist™, will be combined by the Council into a final Cumulative Score which will determine your credentialing decision.

Earn Your CDA® Credential

After the Council receives the scores for both your CDA Verification Visit® and your CDA Exam, the Council creates a Cumulative Score in order to determine your final credentialing decision.

- **Earn your CDA® Credential**
- **Renew your CDA® Credential**
- **Earn a second CDA® Credential**

The Cumulative Score takes into account your understanding of the six CDA Competency Standards and 13 Functional Areas (Part 2 of this book) and your ability to put them into practice. There is not a passing or failing score on either the CDA Exam or the CDA Verification Visit. Rather, the Council comprehensively evaluates how you score in each of the Functional Areas during the CDA Verification Visit and on the CDA Exam to arrive at its decision. As a result, you will not receive a score after you have taken your CDA Exam or after the CDA Verification Visit.

If the Council determines that your Cumulative Score meets the credentialing requirement, you will be awarded the Child Development Associate® (CDA) Credential™. If the Council determines that your Cumulative Score does not meet the credentialing requirement, the Council will notify you and inform you of appeal procedures and other subsequent options.

If you earn your CDA, the Council will mail your credential to the address listed on your application.

Renew Your Credential

A CDA® Credential is valid for three years from the date of award. You may apply to renew your CDA Credential six months before it expires. In order to renew your CDA Credential you will need to provide:

- Proof of your valid and current certificates of completion or cards from a) any Face-to-Face first aid course and b) an infant/child (pediatric) CPR course offered by a nationally-recognized training organization (such as American Red Cross or the American Heart Association). ***Online training is not accepted.**

- Proof of professional education training specific to **original** credential setting: at least 4.5 Continuing Education Units (CEUs) or a three-credit-hour course in early childhood education/child development (these hours must be completed after original 120 clock hours you obtained in order to earn your initial CDA Credential.

- Proof of a minimum of 80 hours of recent work experience with young children specific to the original credential setting (within the current year).

- A completed recommendation form from an early childhood professional regarding your current skills in working with young children specific to the original credential setting (this form can be found in the *CDA® Renewal Procedures Guide*, which is available for download from our website.)

- Proof of current membership in a national or local early childhood professional organization

To learn more about CDA Renewal or view the *CDA® Renewal Procedures Guide*, please visit *www.cdacouncil.org/renewal*.

Earn a Second Credential

Candidates wishing to earn a CDA® Credential of another type (Infant/Toddler, Preschool, Family Child Care or Home Visitor) must complete the CDA credentialing process again. All steps must be completed and you must submit a new assessment fee. However, to meet the requirement of 120 hours of professional education, you may re-use the portions of your professional education that relate to the second credential type (for example, a class titled "Working with Families" could be re-used for any credential type whereas a class titled "Infant Emotional Development" could not be re-used for the Preschool CDA Credential).

Language Specializations

Bilingual Language Specialization (English and a Second Language)

A bilingual program is a child development program that has specific goals for promoting bilingual development in children, in which two languages are consistently used in daily activities and in which families are helped to understand the goals and support children's bilingual development.

A bilingual Candidate is a Candidate who works in this type of program and is required to use both languages daily and consistently with children and their families and who is able to speak, read and write both languages well enough to understand and be understood by others in both English and the second language.

In addition to all of the competencies being assessed in the standard credentialing process, Candidates seeking Bilingual Specialization are also assessed in their ability to promote and facilitate children's bilingual development through consistent use of both languages in daily activities, as required by her/his job in a bilingual program.

Although there is no specific model of bilingual education that this Candidate should follow, a competent Candidate is knowledgeable about the development of language, bilingual communication, and the integration of culture and language. The Candidate should have specific strategies for achieving bilingual development and be able to implement them through consistent daily opportunities where children build on their first language and culture, while learning the second language. This may include programs where children who speak English are learning a second language.

 **Prepare**

Since being added to the CDA® credentialing process in 1979, the CDA Bilingual assessment requirements have been developed so that Candidates working in bilingual programs could demonstrate their special competencies in order to earn a CDA Credential with a Bilingual Specialization. Special, required bilingual examples of competence are now woven into 11 of the 13 Functional Areas, with the exception of "Healthy" and "Physical". The examples are not inclusive - Candidates may think of many additional examples of competent behavior for bilingual early care and learning professionals.

Education Requirements

Candidates applying for Bilingual Specialization are required to study Principles of Dual Language Learning (pp. 109-115) as part of their hours of study under Subject Area #2:"Advancing children's physical and intellectual development". Therefore, in addition to providing verification of completion of 120 clock hours of education in the form of a transcript, certificate or letter, these Candidates must include a course description or syllabus specific and pertinent to a Principles of Dual Language Learning course of study.

The Professional Portfolio

In addition to meeting all of the standard requirements for Professional Portfolios, Bilingual Specialization requires:

Family Questionnaires

When inviting families to complete the Family Questionnaires, families should be asked to complete all questions, paying particular attention to Question #14, which is specific to bilingual programs.

The Resource Collection

The resources used directly with children and families must be presented in both languages (RC I-3, RC II, RC III, RC IV)

Reflective Statements of Competence

Three statements must be written in English and three in the other language (the Candidate may select which ones). All six Statements of Competence must include information in regards to how Candidate applies principles of Dual Language Learning to her bilingual daily practice with children.

Professional Philosophy Statement

The Candidate may write the Professional Philosophy Statement in either language.

 **2 Apply**

Candidates who wish to apply for a Bilingual Specialization may purchase and utilize either the Spanish or English version of this *Competency Standards* book. The Spanish version of this book includes an application, the Comprehensive Scoring Instrument and all resources written in Spanish. At this time, the Council does not offer these materials in other languages.

# ③ Demonstrate

The CDA Verification Visit®

The Candidate must utilize a CDA Professional Development (PD) Specialist™ who is proficient in both languages (able to speak, read and write English and the other language) and can understand and be understood by both children and adults. The PD Specialist must have direct experience with Bilingual Early Childhood programs and with non-English speaking populations. The PD Specialist will conduct the reflective dialogue with the Candidate in both languages.

The Observation held during the CDA Verification Visit must take place in an eligible bilingual program and must reflect the Candidate's work using both languages daily and consistently.

 Candidates seeking Bilingual Specialization must also display competence in additional required examples found throughout the *Competency Standards* as denoted by the special icon on the left.

The CDA® Exam

The CDA Exam may be taken by all Candidates in either English or Spanish. Candidates applying for a Bilingual Specialization of English and a language other than Spanish will take the Exam in English.

Monolingual Language Specialization

In addition to meeting all of the standard requirements for earning the CDA® Credential, Candidates applying for a Monolingual Specialization must meet the following requirements. Note: If the language of the Specialization is other than Spanish, the Candidate must contact the Council before applying in order to discuss special arrangements.

① Prepare

The Professional Portfolio

In addition to meeting all of the standard requirements for Professional Portfolios, Monolingual Specialization requires:

Family Questionnaires

Family Questionnaires may be completed in either language by families.

The Resource Collection

The resources used directly with children and families must be presented in Spanish (RC I-3, RC II, RC III, RC IV)

Reflective Statements of Competence

All statements must be written in Spanish.

Professional Philosophy Statement

The Candidate must write the Professional Philosophy Statement in Spanish.

③ Demonstrate

The CDA Verification Visit®

The Candidate must select a CDA Professional Development (PD) Specialist™ who is proficient in Spanish.

The Observation must take place in an eligible monolingual setting and must reflect the Candidate's work using Spanish language daily and consistently

The PD Specialist will conduct the reflective dialogue with the Candidate in Spanish.

The CDA® Exam

The CDA Exam may be taken by all Candidates, including Monolingual Candidates, in either English or Spanish. Candidates applying for a Monolingual Specialization in a language other than Spanish must contact the Council for special arrangements.

Part

The Child Development Associate® Competency Standards

I. To establish and maintain a safe, healthy learning environment

II. To advance physical and intellectual competence

III. To support social and emotional development and provide positive guidance

IV. To establish positive and productive relationships with families

V. To ensure a well-run, purposeful program that is responsive to participant needs

VI. To maintain a commitment to professionalism

The Child Development Associate® Competency Standards

Candidates seeking to earn the CDA Credential are assessed based upon the CDA Competency Standards. These national standards are the criteria used to evaluate an early care and learning professional's performance with children, families, colleagues and their community.

There are six *Competency Standards* - statements that set the standard of competency for professional behavior. The first four Standards relate directly to the experiences of young children and are therefore presented within a *Developmental Context*. Each Developmental Context presents a brief overview of relevant child development principles related to the Functional Areas within that Standard.

The six Standards are then defined in more detail in 13 *Functional Areas*, which describe the major tasks or functions that an early care and learning professional must complete in order to meet each Competency Standard. Each Functional Area includes *Items* that further define it as well as *Indicators* that further delineate each Item. Additionally, most Items have a list of optional *Examples* to further illustrate key professional practices. The Examples are not intended to be all-inclusive as individual teaching styles, cultural norms and program needs vary. It is likely that Candidates, CDA CDA Professional Development (PD) Specialists™ and other readers may think of many more examples, in addition to the ones listed.

Examples have also been provided for certain Items that are unique to Bilingual Specialization. Please refer to "Principles for Dual Language Learners" (pp. 109-115) for additional principles that provide guidance for working with preschool children whose primary (home) language is not English. A description of the developmental components of dual language acquisition emphasizes the importance of competent practices that support constructive dual language development of preschool children. Multiple examples of competent practice are presented.

Competent early care and learning professionals integrate their work and constantly adapt their skills, always thinking of the development of the whole child. In all Functional Areas, it is important for these professionals to individualize their work with each child while meeting the needs of the group. Additionally, professionals must display cultural competence, supporting children and families of varied cultural groups as well as meeting the unique needs of children with special needs. Competent professionals must also demonstrate personal qualities, such as flexibility and a positive style of communicating with young children and working with families.

Navigating the CDA® Competency Standards

Universal Standards

The Standards, Functional Areas, Items and Indicators are universal (i.e, they apply to Infant/Toddler, Preschool and Family Child Care settings). However, the Examples are based on children's developmental levels and may vary by Credential type (in other words, some of the Preschool examples found in this book may be different than the infant/toddler examples found in the *Infant/Toddler Competency Standards* book).

Hierarchy of the Standards

Key to the Hierarchy of the CDA Competency Standards:

Competency Standard

Functional Area

Item/Item/Item

a) Indicator

• Example

Organization of Items

For ease-of use by the CDA Professional Development (PD) Specialist™, the Items on the following pages have been color-coded to match the way they will be reviewed and observed using the Comprehensive Scoring Instrument at the back of this book:

Settings & Activities

Actions & Interactions

Review

Bilingual Specialization

 Indicates a required example for Candidates seeking Bilingual Specialization

Preschool Competency Standards At-A-Glance

Competency Standard	Functional Area	Definitions
I. To establish and maintain a safe, healthy learning environment	**1. Safe**	Candidate provides a safe environment and teaches children safe practices to prevent and reduce injuries.
	2. Healthy	Candidate provides an environment that promotes health and prevents illness, and teaches children about good nutrition and practices that promote wellness.
	3. Learning Environment	Candidate organizes and uses relationships, the physical space, materials, daily schedule, and routines to create a secure, interesting, and enjoyable environment that promotes engagement, play, exploration, and learning of all children including children with special needs.
II. To advance physical and intellectual competence	**4. Physical**	Candidate uses a variety of developmentally appropriate equipment, learning experiences and teaching strategies to promote the physical development (fine motor and gross motor) of all children.
	5. Cognitive	Candidate uses a variety of developmentally appropriate learning experiences and teaching strategies to promote curiosity, reasoning, and problem solving and to lay the foundation for all later learning. Candidate implements curriculum that promotes children's learning of important mathematics, science, technology, social studies and other content goals.
	6. Communication	Candidate uses a variety of developmentally appropriate learning experiences and teaching strategies to promote children's language and early literacy learning, and help them communicate their thoughts and feelings verbally and nonverbally. Candidate helps dual-language learners make progress in understanding and speaking both English and their home language.
	7. Creative	Candidate uses a variety of developmentally appropriate learning experiences and teaching strategies for children to explore music, movement, and the visual arts, and to develop and express their individual creative abilities.
III. To support social and emotional development and to provide positive guidance	**8. Self**	Candidate develops a warm, positive, supportive, and responsive relationship with each child, and helps each child learn about and take pride in his or her individual and cultural identity.
	9. Social	Candidate helps each child function effectively in the group, learn to express feelings, acquire social skills, and make friends, and promotes mutual respect among children and adults.
	10. Guidance	Candidate provides a supportive environment and uses effective strategies to promote children's self-regulation and support acceptable behaviors, and effectively intervenes for children with persistent challenging behaviors.
IV. To establish positive and productive relationships with families	**11. Families**	Candidate establishes a positive, responsive, and cooperative relationship with each child's family, engages in two-way communication with families, encourages their involvement in the program, and supports the child's relationship with his or her family.
V. To ensure a well-run, purposeful program that is responsive to participant needs	**12. Program Management**	Candidate is a manager who uses observation, documentation, and planning to support children's development and learning and to ensure effective operation of the classroom or group. The Candidate is a competent organizer, planner, record keeper, communicator, and a cooperative co-worker.
VI. To maintain a commitment to professionalism	**13. Professionalism**	Candidate makes decisions based on knowledge of research-based early childhood practices, promotes high-quality in child care services, and takes advantage of opportunities to improve knowledge and competence, both for personal and professional growth and for the benefit of children and families.

Competency Standard I:

To establish and maintain a safe, healthy learning environment

Developmental Contexts

Safe: Preschool children (3 through 5 years old) are gradually able to understand the relative danger or safety of situations. In a safe environment, children will gradually learn to protect themselves and look out for others.

Healthy: Preschool children are ready to learn the reasons and take responsibility for good health practices including hygiene, hand washing and good nutrition. They are fascinated by their own bodily functions and can gradually learn about them.

Learning Environment: Preschool children are developing new language skills, physical control, and awareness of themselves and others each day. They enjoy participation in planned and group activities, but they are not yet ready to sit still or work in a group for very long. They learn by doing. Adults can support their learning in all areas by maintaining an environment that is dependable but flexible enough to provide opportunities for them to extend their skills, understanding and judgment in individualized ways. Adults can observe children's play, give them time and space to repeat familiar activities and expand the learning environment in response to their developing skills, interests and concerns about themselves and their world.

Functional Area 1: Safe

Candidate provides a safe environment and teaches children safe practices to prevent and reduce injuries.

Item 1.1 Environments are safe for all children and adults.

Indicator:

a) **Materials, equipment and environments are safe**

Examples

- Indoor and outdoor play areas are in good repair, free of debris, structural hazards, splinters, unguarded space heaters, tools, etc.

- Dangerous substances are not in children's reach (such as anything labeled "keep out of reach of children," medicine, cleaning products, matches, chipping paint, toxic plants, small objects that could be swallowed, balloons and plastic bags)

- Indoor and outdoor playground equipment is cushioned with pads or other materials thick enough to prevent injuries

- Toys and equipment meet current safety standards

- Safety equipment (such as fire extinguishers and smoke detectors) is in place and operable

- All children's materials are non-toxic, non-flammable and/or water-based

- Furnishings are appropriate for children's development and size

- Outlets are covered with safety caps or other safety devices

- Cords on electronics and window coverings are out of children's reach

- Heating or a/c units are secured and/or inaccessible to children

- Walls and furniture do not have sharp edges

- Rugs and all carpeting lie flat, have non-skid backing or are secured to the floor where necessary

- Exits are properly marked and unobstructed

- Safety goggles are available for use with woodworking

1.2 Well-planned and well-organized emergency procedures and supplies are evident.

a) Procedures for fires and other emergencies are posted

Examples

- A list of current phone numbers for contacting parents and emergency services (poison control, fire stations, police, ambulance/medical help) is accessible

- Posted emergency instructions use diagrams, pictures and words to effectively convey procedures to children, families and staff

- A written evacuation plan is posted

b) First-aid supplies and medicines are stored appropriately and accessible to adults only

Examples

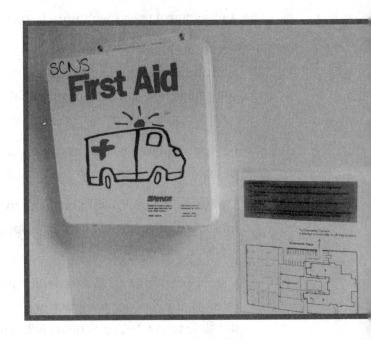

- A first aid kit is evident in the classroom

- A portable first aid kit is available to be taken to the playground and on neighborhood walks, field trips

- Unique first aid equipment and medicines are available for authorized children (such as an EpiPen for children with asthma)

- Medicines are labeled and stored as indicated, out-of-reach of children

1.3 Candidate ensures children's safety at all times.

a) Ensures that children are attended by authorized adults at all times

Examples

- Does not leave children alone with an unauthorized adult

- Knows basic first aid and CPR procedures appropriate for young children (for example, how to handle choking or treating cuts)

- Releases each child only to authorized individuals

b) Teaches children appropriate safety practices

Examples

- Teaches how to safely use equipment (climbing structures, ride on toys, lofts)

- Talks with children about "good touch" and "bad touch" as a way of preventing sexual abuse

- Regularly practices effective procedures for fires and other emergencies, including safety procedures for children with disabilities

- Models safety practices and gives step-by-step explanations of what and why the practices are necessary and effective

- Teaches children simple safety rules and enforces rules consistently

- Talks and role plays with preschoolers about safety precautions

- Involves children in setting basic safety rules, discussing with children why a rule is needed, what might happen if children forget to follow the rule and how the rule will keep them safe, using visual and verbal reminders to help children remember each rule

- Reviews and discusses safety rules and practices before a potentially hazardous activity or experience (such as a cooking activity or neighborhood walk)

- Discusses the use of safe practices in context, such as when the children are using a knife to slice a banana or when stopping at the corner to watch for traffic before crossing the street

- Uses teachable moments to demonstrate or explain, in simple language, cause and effect/natural consequences (for example "If you don't wait for another child on the slide to get off, you could slide right into him" or "If you climb on the table, you may fall and hurt yourself")

 Candidates seeking Bilingual Specialization must also show evidence of the following:

- Explains to and practices with each child in their second language safety procedures such as fire drills

c) Provides attentive supervision at all times

Examples

- Supervises all children's activities indoors and outdoors

- Takes safety precautions in a reassuring manner without making children fearful

- Handles emergencies in a reassuring manner without making children fearful

- Uses safe auto and bus travel procedures, including appropriate use of car seats and/or safety belts

- Anticipates and makes plans to prevent potentially dangerous situations, such as children being left alone or separated while on a field trip

d) Makes sure foods that are known choking hazards are not served

Example

- Small foods that may cause choking (such as hot dog or other cut-up meat pieces, grapes, popcorn, nuts, marshmallows, gummi candies, hard candies, seeds, cherries, etc.) are not served

Functional Area 2: Healthy

Candidate provides an environment that promotes health, prevents illness and teaches children about good nutrition and practices that promote wellness.

Item 2.1 Children's settings promote good health.

Indicator:

a) Materials, equipment and environments are clean and promote good health

Examples

- Play areas and materials are clean

- Covered, plastic-lined containers are available for used tissues, diapers or other biohazards

b) Disinfecting and sanitizing solutions are present and stored appropriately

Examples

- Chemical air fresheners and scented products are not used

- Bleach/water solution is used to disinfect and sanitize surfaces and materials

- Cleaning supplies are stored in dated, labeled containers, out of children's reach and separated from foods and medicines

c) Relevant health information from families of children are maintained and posted

Examples

- Children's current food allergies are posted (when applicable)

- Current emergency telephone numbers for each child's parent(s), nearest relative, and medical providers are easily accessible

- Health records, medication and first aid administration procedures/forms are available

2.2 Candidate implements appropriate hygiene practices to minimize the spread of infectious diseases.

a) Cleans/sanitizes materials and equipment

Examples

- Wipes down all surfaces used by children (tables, furniture, countertops, etc.)

- Sweeps/mops floors

- Follows procedures for cleaning, sanitizing, and disinfecting toys and materials

b) Uses correct hand washing procedures before and after serving food, diapering/toileting and whenever needed

Examples

- Follows proper hand washing sequence: wets hands, adds liquid soap, washes for twenty seconds, rinses, dries, turns off water using paper towel

- Washes hands before and after toileting, food preparation, eating, wiping noses and after coming into contact with any bodily fluids

c) Implements sanitary toileting procedures

Examples

- Seals soiled clothes in labeled plastic bags

- Provides extra clothes for children when their clothes become soiled

- Ensures that toilet facilities are sanitary; toilets are flushed after each use; spills of bodily fluids are cleaned with bleach solution

2.3 Candidate encourages children to practice healthy habits.

a) Ensures that children wash hands properly, with assistance when needed

Examples

- Facilitates children's hand washing and toileting activities in a positive, relaxed, and pleasant atmosphere

- Teaches proper hand washing sequence: wet hands, add soap, wash for twenty seconds, rinse, dry, turn off water using paper towel

- Models proper hand washing techniques

- Provides a step stool when necessary so that children can wash hands when they are capable

b) Models, communicates and provides activities that teach the importance of good health to children and families

Examples

- Ensures that children wear clothing appropriate for the weather, providing extra clothing as needed

- Recognizes unusual behavior and changes in each child's physical health, encouraging parents to obtain appropriate treatment when needed

- Ensures that children do not share personal items (such as hairbrushes, combs, etc.)

- Enacts procedures for care of sick children (for example, isolates a child with a contagious illness from well children while maintaining supervision, contacts parents and medical providers)

- Uses roleplaying, modeling, visual materials and real objects to teach healthy physical, mental, dental and nutritional practices

- Provides opportunities for children to learn about health care by talking about visits to the doctor and dentist, reading books and encouraging pretend play about health care

- Models how to sneeze into elbow to avoid the spread of germs

- Recognizes the signs of a health crisis that children with special needs may have and responds appropriately (for example, seizures)

- Plans activities that integrate health and nutrition information from the children's cultural groups with medically accepted health and nutrition practices

- Communicates to children and their parents the importance of outdoor play and physical activity for healthy growth and development

2.4 Candidate provides appropriate mealtime experiences.

a) Serves nutritious meals and snacks

Examples

- Plans age-appropriate, nutritious menus, meals and snacks that are culturally familiar to children

- Limits sugar, salt, processed foods, unnecessary chemical additives, and artificial coloring/flavoring in meals and snacks

- Serves natural, unsweetened fruits, juices and jams/preserves

- Promotes drinking water over sugared drinks

- Includes a variety of fresh fruits and vegetables in meals/snacks

- Ensures that lunches and snacks brought for one child are not shared with other children

- Shares nutrition information with families, encouraging them to provide healthy foods when they contribute food to the program

b) Facilitates appropriate mealtime experiences

Examples

- Establishes a relaxed mealtime routine that makes eating pleasant for each child

- Provides appropriate amounts of food to children

- Encourages children to feed themselves

- Respects children's food choices

- Does not require children to finish food on their plates

- Does not use meals/snacks as rewards or punishments

- Facilitates "Family-Style Dining"

- Encourages pleasant table conversations

- Ensures that children eat while seated rather than when walking, running, playing or lying down

Functional Area 3: Learning Environment

Candidate organizes and uses relationships, the physical space, materials, daily schedule and routines to create a secure, interesting and enjoyable environment that promotes engagement, play, exploration and learning of all children, including children with disabilities and special needs.

Item 3.1 Environments are developmentally appropriate for young children.

Indicator:

a) Environments are pleasant, welcoming and provide appropriate levels of stimulation

Examples

- Environments are "home-like"

- Pleasing, culturally-diverse posters or pictures are on display

- No or few commercial characters are displayed

- Children's art, culturally relevant objects and/or plants/items from nature are present

- Bright colors and visual clutter are minimized

- Music is played at a comfortable level

- Music playing reflects children's interests and cultural groups

- A "private" space for children to be on their own is provided (book corner, cardboard box/barrel, tent, etc.)

b) Environments are arranged and organized intentionally to meet the developmental needs of children

Examples

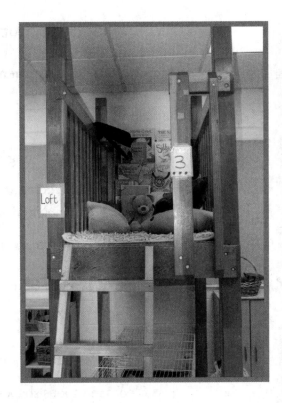

- Room arrangement encourages participation and interaction of all children, including those with special needs

- Quiet areas (such as the book, art or writing centers) are positioned next to each other, separated from noisier and more active areas (such as blocks or pretend play)

- Environments are designed to help children succeed (for example, block building has enough space and is protected from traffic; areas such as long corridors or large, open spaces that invite children's running or fighting are kept to a minimum)

- Messy activities such as sand/water play and art are located near a source of water for easy cleanup

- Spaces, materials and equipment are provided inside and outside for child-initiated exploration

- Environments are "print-rich," exposing children to the written word at their eye level (such as meaningful signs, labeled shelves and containers, books, etc.)

- Children's art work is displayed respectfully

- Sufficient space is provided for creating and storing completed work and work-in-progress

- A transition area at the entrance of the room provides families with a space to drop off and pick up children and their belongings

- Spaces are adapted as needed for children with special needs

- Learning areas include books, sensory discovery, blocks, pretend play, art, music, writing, science, quiet/library, manipulatives, woodworking (for older preschoolers)

- Learning centers are divided using furniture, floor coverings or shelves that help limit the number of children who work or play in each at one time

- Environments and materials include different opportunities for exploration (such as soft/hard, open-ended/closed-ended, quiet/active, messy/neat, pretend/real)

• A comfortable meeting space is provided for the whole group to engage in music, movement, book reading and other large group activities; seating is arranged so that children are not crowded or distracted by items within reach

3.2 Developmentally appropriate materials are available.

a) Materials are developmentally appropriate for all children

Examples

• Materials are engaging, challenging children without being too easy

• Materials used demonstrate acceptance of each child's gender, family, race, language, religion and cultural groups

• Materials are modified to support the needs of all children

b) A variety of materials are provided for children to explore

Examples

• Toys and equipment from easily available materials are used in the classroom

• Blocks in various shapes and sizes; a variety of manipulatives; sand/water play; pegboards; beads to string; construction sets; things for children to count/sort; puzzles; dress-up supplies; objects of many textures; cause/effect materials; open-ended materials are provided

• Digital media is used in a developmentally appropriate way to support and extend learning across the curriculum

c) There is a sufficient number of materials to accommodate the group size

Examples

• Extra materials are available and rotated into play as children's needs and interests change

• Duplicates of the most popular materials are provided

d) Materials are organized and accessible to children throughout the day

Examples

- Materials are sorted and placed at children's level

- New materials are offered/rotated regularly

- Shelves are labeled with words/pictures

3.3   Daily schedule and weekly plan(s) are developmentally appropriate.

a) Schedule allows for routine needs of children to be met

Examples

- Daily schedule reflects times each day for children's personal needs such as eating/drinking, resting, toileting, etc.

- Provides enough time for children to successfully accomplish routine tasks (such as putting on jackets or shoes, etc.)

- Consistent routines throughout the day balance active and quiet, free and structured, indoor and outdoor activities

 Candidates seeking Bilingual Specialization must also show evidence of the following:

- Establishes and maintains a routine for use of the second language in daily activities

b) Schedule provided meets children's needs for play

Example

- Center/Free Choice Times last 75 minutes (In a full-day program, at least 60 minutes are provided both in the morning and the afternoon.)

c) Whole group times, when offered, are developmentally appropriate

Examples

- Group Times last as long as children display interest

- Group Times provide many engaging opportunities for active, sensory-oriented learning

d) Weekly plans provide a variety of experiences

Examples

- Weekly plans utilize observational data in order to support goals for both individual and groups of children

- Schedule provides a balance of learning experiences: large group, small group, and individualized; child-initiated/led and teacher-initiated/led; active and quiet; structured and unstructured

- Weekly plans include interactions with the community when possible; for example, short trips to local shops, walks around the block, community events

- Activities provide many opportunities for children to interact with each other and the natural world, develop their senses, use their bodies and stimulate their interests

- Activities include child-initiated, small and large group activities

- "Messy" activities , such as water and sand play, finger painting and drawing with markers, are planned

- Process-oriented activities are offered more often than activities intended to create products

- A variety of activities are provided that reflect the cultural groups of the children in the classroom community

~ Candidates seeking Bilingual Specialization must also show evidence of the following:

- Uses knowledge of second language development to plan for each child and the group

- Encourages learning in both languages through everyday experiences and activities

- Knows families' views on relevant issues (such as the use of first and second languages within the program, childrearing and biculturalism) and incorporates their views into planning

- Lullabies, songs, games, stories, books and finger plays from both languages are used, asking parents for familiar examples

e) Pleasant nap or quiet times meet children's needs for rest

Examples

- Provides soothing naptime routines (such as book-reading or storytelling)

- Sings lullabies as their backs are gently rubbed

- Children are allowed to hold a security object while resting

- Creates an environment of love and trust through warm and responsive caring

- Preschoolers have at least one rest/nap each day for full-day program; quiet time each day for half-day programs

3.4 Candidate's disposition is warm and respectful.

a) Creates a nurturing relationship with each child

Examples

- Smiles often

- Is upbeat/excited or serious, as appropriate

- Delights in each child's successes

- Expresses kindness and support when a child is having trouble

- Has appropriate physical contact with each child daily in ways that convey love, affection and security

- Uses warm voice, body language and facial expressions with all children

- Talks with and listens to children at their eye level (such as on the floor when reading and at children's table when eating)

- Enjoys children's senses of humor

- Responds immediately and sympathetically to a child's injury or fear of injury, encouraging caring responses by the other children

3.5 Candidate demonstrates sound judgment in using the posted Weekly Schedule/Daily Plan.

a) Generally follows posted schedule and plan

b) Veers from schedule and plan as needed

Examples

- Embraces "teachable moments" or other learning opportunities when they arise (stays on playground longer when children find a worm or bug of interest, extends time for an activity when children continue to display high interest levels)

- Varies routines spontaneously to take advantage of unusual opportunities (for example, goes outside in the snow, invites a visiting grandmother to share stories or songs, invites

the children to watch workers and machinery on the street, plays with one child for an extended amount of time when enough adults are available to care for the group)

- Adapts the daily plan to accommodate individual children's needs and interests, including children with special needs

- Gives children time to finish activities before transitioning to next activity

- Adjusts Group Time activity if not working well

3.6 Candidate effectively facilitates transitional times between activities.

a) Uses a variety of strategies to transition children from one activity to another

Examples

- Intentionally uses songs, movement, games to engage children's interests or learning throughout each transition (for example, by singing songs, reciting rhymes or poems, counting steps, following the leader's motions, doing movement exercises, or following specific directions such as, "If your name starts with a K, get your coat.")

- Prepares for the next activity so that children do not spend excessive amounts of time waiting

- Transitions occur in a planned, predictable manner

- Alerts children to changes in routine or upcoming transitions well in advance (such as "Five more minutes until Cleanup Time!")

- For those children who have particular difficulty with transitions, gives them an individual warning and explanation of what is to come

- Individualizes transitions from one activity to another with clear directions and patience

- Minimizes the number of transitions between activities

- Minimizes the amount of time children spend in transitions

Competency Standard II:

To advance physical and intellectual competence

Developmental Contexts

Physical: Preschool children (3 through 5 years old) are gradually refining new skills: skipping, drawing, threading, throwing and catching. They are interested in learning subtle differences through their senses: sweet and sour, rough and smooth, high and low, loud and soft. They can attend and persist for longer periods of time when they are absorbed in using their small muscles on a puzzle or an art project. They also need daily opportunities to exercise their large muscles in free play and organized activities. Daily physical activities can promote children's cognitive, creative, and language growth as well as their physical development.

Cognitive: Preschool children continue their cognitive development by actively exploring their world and manipulating objects, thinking and solving problems, talking and engaging with adults and other children in a variety of roles and repeating and practicing their learning. Their increasing ability to describe objects and experiences with words reinforces their understanding of abstract concepts. Adults can expand learning through play, introduce a variety of new opportunities for learning and ensure that preschoolers experience a balance of challenge and success.

Communication: Preschool children develop a wide range of abilities to communicate both verbally and nonverbally. Adults should communicate actively with each child — modeling good speech, listening carefully, responding actively to their expressions, engaging in conversations with them, and building on their verbal and nonverbal understanding and vocabulary. During the preschool years, early literacy experiences provide the foundation for later success in learning to read and write.

Creative: Preschool children can express their creativity in increasingly symbolic ways through the use of their bodies, words, and materials (building blocks, music, dance, art) and through make-believe. Adults can promote creativity by providing space, time, and materials for children to create and recreate their individual works, their own dramas, and their unique solutions to problems and by respecting the process of creativity as much as the product.

Functional Area 4: Physical

Candidate uses a variety of developmentally appropriate equipment, learning experiences and teaching strategies to promote the physical development (fine motor and gross motor) of all children.

Item 4.1 Activities, materials and equipment encourage children of varying abilities to develop their large muscles.

Indicator:

a) **Gross motor skills are encouraged through developmentally appropriate materials, equipment and indoor/outdoor activities**

Examples

- Preschoolers have safe opportunities to walk, run, climb, jump, throw, kick, dance, gallop, balance, rock, ride, push, pedal, etc.

- A variety of activities are offered to preschoolers that reflect their cultural groups, such as dances, music/movement and active games

- Preschoolers are provided with materials such as scarves, bean bags, balls, ribbons, etc.

- Structured activities are offered that introduce a variety of movement skills with a partner or in a small group (for example, may offer balls of different sizes and materials - rubber, foam, inflatable - to roll, kick, throw, or catch

- Activities are offered that encourage children to practice balancing

4.2 Activities and materials encourage children of varying abilities to develop their small muscles.

a) Individual fine motor skills are encouraged through a variety of developmentally appropriate materials and activities

Examples

- Preschoolers have materials that support a range of fine motor skill levels (such as a variety of manipulatives, puzzles of varying complexity, etc.)

- Preschoolers have opportunities to use utensils/tools (for example, a spoon to stir, a funnel to pour water through, a container to fill with and carry objects, a shovel to scoop sand)

- Preschoolers use a variety of writing/drawing/painting instruments

- Preschoolers use safety scissors, puppets, play dough, manipulatives, sorting objects, toys with zippers/buttons/clasps, lacing beads/boards, etc.

- Everyday routines provide children with opportunities to develop fine motor skills (for example, folding napkins, putting on and taking off coats, hats, and boots, mixing paints, washing paintbrushes, pouring from small pitchers)

4.3 Activities and materials encourage children to develop their senses.

a) Sight, sound, smell, taste and touch experiences are encouraged through a variety of developmentally appropriate materials and activities

Examples

- Activities offered include opportunities to notice colors, smell scents, distinguish sounds, feel and touch a variety of textures, taste different foods, listen to music from around the world, etc.

- Materials offered include texture boards, smell jars, scented playdough, musical instruments, matching/patterning games, etc.

4.4 Candidate's facilitation promotes children's physical development.

a) Participates in physical activities with children, when appropriate

Examples

- Initiates or joins in dancing, game playing, climbing, drawing, painting, etc.

- Ensures that all children are well-supervised before joining in an activity

b) Guides the development of children's fine and gross motor skills

Examples

- Offers individualized assistance, learning how children approach and respond to physical challenges

- Encourages children to practice and refine their skills

- Supports and encourages, but does not force, children who are fearful of physical activity

- Offers challenges that will help the child progress without getting frustrated

- Models movement and motor skills (for example, how to hold a hammer, use scissors, walk on a balance beam, etc.)

- Adapts learning experiences to allow children with different levels of motor skills and children with special needs to participate with success (for example, while making a group collage, children who are not able to cut pieces of paper, may tear the paper; while tossing a ball, children who are having a hard time stand closer to the target)

- Gives instructions/demonstrates/facilitates cutting with scissors, zipping up coats, tying shoes, throwing/catching a ball

- Avoids overprotecting children with special needs, supports their independent functioning, and includes them in physical activities with other children (making modifications only when necessary)

Functional Area 5: Cognitive

Candidate uses a variety of developmentally appropriate learning experiences and teaching strategies to promote curiosity, reasoning and problem-solving to lay the foundation for all later learning. Candidate implements curriculum that promotes children's learning of important mathematics, science, technology, social studies and other content goals.

Item 5.1 Activities encourage curiosity, exploration and discovery.

Indicator:

a) Activities involve developmentally appropriate, hands-on experiences

Examples

• Children are provided time for active play and exploration

• Children learn through active experiences

• Engaging activities are meaningful to children's interests

• Activities spark children's natural curiosity

• Experiences for each child are developmentally appropriate

• A variety of activities are provided to introduce young children to math, science, technology, social studies and other curricular disciplines

• Experiences provided reflect the range of the children's cultural groups

• Activities target concepts such as prediction, estimation, classification, sorting, patterning, sequencing, cause and effect, counting, spatial awareness, ordering/grouping, comparing/contrasting, etc.

• Children are provided the opportunity for deeper explorations of topics of interest through extended projects

Candidates seeking Bilingual Specialization must also show evidence of the following:

- Provides learning experiences that lead to the understanding of basic concepts in the language most familiar to each child

5.2 Materials and equipment stimulate children's thinking and problem-solving.

a) Materials and equipment provide a variety of opportunities for cognitive development

Examples

- Children are provided a variety of objects to inspect and manipulate to develop an understanding of how they work

- Puzzles, books, manipulatives, water/sand play are provided

- Blocks are developmentally appropriate and varied

- Materials and equipment are modified for individual children as needed

- Materials provided introduce young children to math, science, technology, social studies and other curricular disciplines

- Children are provided "real" science items like worms, leaves, sticks, rocks, shells, scales, magnifying glasses, etc.

- Materials provided encourage children's inventive thinking

b) Materials chosen are meaningful to the children

Examples

- Materials reflect interests expressed by the children

- Materials build on and extend children's interest in the natural world and living things

- Materials reflect children's cultural groups and languages

5.3 Candidate's interactions promote children's thinking and problem solving.

a) Facilitates children's thinking and creative problem-solving skills

Examples

- Listens to children and encourages them to think/talk about what they see, hear, smell, taste and touch

- Models curiosity, inquiry, and investigation for children

- Encourages children to ask questions and seek help, responding to them in ways that extend their thinking; for example, "That's a good question; let's see if we can find out."

- Asks why…/how…/what if… questions (open-ended questions that have many possible answers)

- Helps children notice cause and effect by providing "if this happens, then that will occur" statements and/or questions

- Facilitates children's thinking by giving hints when needed

- Encourages children to wonder, guess, and talk about their ideas

- Incorporates mathematics and science concepts throughout daily activities

- Uses routines such as snack and mealtimes, cleanup, washing hands, dressing for outdoors, or rest time as learning opportunities (sitting and talking with children during meals and snacks) and for children to practice newly acquired skills

- Helps children discover ways to solve problems that arise in daily activities (such as how to put on a jacket, how to pour a pitcher of water or how to walk safely together through the neighborhood, etc.)

- Encourages active learning, rather than emphasizing that children listen passively to adults

5.4 Candidate's interactions intentionally build upon children's prior knowledge.

a) Connects concepts to children's previous experiences

Examples

- Builds on and extends children's knowledge and understanding of their world

- Listens to children and intentionally expands their ideas when appropriate

b) Supports children's repetition of the familiar

Examples

- Supports children's desire to repeat tasks that are familiar to them as they practice new skills

- Regularly re-reads popular/frequently-requested books

- Provides materials so that children can repeat and practice on their own

Functional Area 6: Communication

Candidate uses a variety of developmentally appropriate learning experiences and teaching strategies to promote children's language and early literacy learning. Candidate helps them communicate their thoughts and feelings verbally and nonverbally. Candidate helps dual-language learners make progress in understanding and speaking both English and their home language.

Item 6.1 Materials promote early literacy.

Indicator:

a) Literacy/storytelling/bookmaking materials are provided

Examples

- Books in the classroom reflect children's cultural groups, home languages and identities

- Books are attractively displayed on open shelves, in good condition, with covers facing front, accessible to children

- Opportunities for verbal expression are provided through puppets, dolls, pretend play clothes/materials, flannel boards, etc.

- Recordings of favorite books/ stories are provided for children to listen to (if possible, parents record themselves telling favorite stories and singing songs)

- Bookmaking materials are available for children's use (paper, stapler, pencils/ markers/crayons, glue, scissors, magazines, etc.)

- Activities allow children to touch and manipulate letters or words (for example, magnetic or sandpaper letters, writing letters in flour or sand, letter/word games, etc.)

b) Developmentally appropriate books are available

Examples

- An assortment of books is available including fiction, information books, books related to children's interests, books that reflect the many cultural groups and family structures of the children, books that display non-traditional gender roles, tactile books, rhyming books, books with predictable text, books with no words, magazines, etc.

- Books made by the children are included

- Handmade books with pictures of children's families, pets, friends, etc. are included

 Candidates seeking Bilingual Specialization must also show evidence of the following:

- Selects books and other appropriate materials in both languages

6.2 Activities promote language development.

a) Children are read to every day

Examples

- Small groups (4 to 6 children) are read to frequently, allowing for greater individual participation, the use of more complex text and engaging conversations about the book

- Whole group reading is occasionally offered using engaging, predictable books

- Children are offered the opportunity to read or tell stories to the group

- Children are read books in various languages at different times, but not immediately following the English versions

b) Activities advance the development of language acquisition and writing skills

Examples

- Activities promote phonological awareness (such as matching sounds, beginning sounds, ending sounds, letters, words)

- Activities include cross-cultural finger plays, games, books, songs used to tell stories; short poems that children enjoy; telling stories without books, dictating stories, writing in journals

- Activities encourage children to develop listening and comprehension skills (such as telling stories about events that occurred in the children's lives, for example, "Remember when we took a walk to the garden?")

- Activities provide children opportunities to learn the uses of written language (for example, signs, environmental print, labels, newspapers/magazines, family notices, etc.)

- Children write signs or labels using pictures, letter-like symbols, letters and their own "writing"

- Children have time to select their own books to look at alone or with a friend(s)

- Children dictate stories, picture descriptions, chart content or messages to Candidate who writes and reads them back to children

- When dual language learners are present, activities help children begin to understand and use the English language while simultaneously developing their primary (home) language

c) Activities provide frequent opportunities for children to listen, talk and express their ideas effectively

Examples

- Children are encouraged to have frequent, meaningful, extended conversations with adults and other children every day about their experiences and topics of interest

- Activities allow children to represent their ideas nonverbally (for example, storytelling, painting, drawing, music-making, dramatic play, puppet play, dance and creative movement)

- Children are encourage to take turns talking and listening instead of interrupting each other or adults, ensuring that each child has a chance to speak

 Candidates seeking Bilingual Specialization must also show evidence of the following:

- Children have opportunities to express themselves in the language of their choice

d) Activities support the needs of dual language learners (when applicable - see pp. 109-115 for expanded examples)

Examples

- Numerous appropriate experiences help children gain receptive understanding of the new language — specifically, to hear the sounds of the new language and connect them to people, objects and experiences

- Experiences encourage and help children practice sounds and words of the new language, taking into account the stages and patterns of home language and English language acquisition

6.3 Candidate reads to children in a developmentally appropriate manner.

a) Reads to children engagingly

Examples

- Holds book so that all children can see pictures during reading

- Keeps children's attention by holding eye contact, speaking clearly, matching tempo with the book's story, "acting out" the book using character voices, hand/body movements, facial expressions, etc.

- Shows book cover, asking for predictions regarding what the book is about

- Asks questions at key moments (for example, "What do you think will happen next?")

- Extends book-reading experiences with related activities/projects

6.4 Candidate's interactions encourage children's communication skills.

a) Promotes children's language development through her/his verbal and non-verbal communications

Examples

- Frequently invites dialogue/conversations with individual children about subjects meaningful to them

- Talks with children about their experiences and home lives

- Gives clear, understandable answers to children's questions; reflects/expands on what child has said

- Does not dominate conversations; talks only as long as children are interested

- Takes turns when talking with child; talks with, not at, child

- Uses "Self Talk" ("I'm going to make breakfast now. First I'll get out the bread and then I will get the eggs.")

- Elaborates on children's short phrases to help them express intended meaning ("Milk? You want more milk?")

- Models standard grammatical speech

- Models and encourages children's creativity in language; for example, through rhymes, imaginative stories and nonsense words

- Uses varied, attention-grabbing, affectionate and playful tones when appropriate

- Communicates, with eyes and voice, attention and interest to an exploring child at a distance from the caregiver

- Asks questions that challenges each child's growing literacy skills (for example, if a child has been writing his name with just a J, asks, "What comes after J, Jamal?" and shows him the next letter if he doesn't know it)

Candidates seeking Bilingual Specialization must also show evidence of the following:

- Demonstrates ability to understand, speak, read and write both languages

b) Interacts with children, listening and responding appropriately

Examples

- Listens to children with respect, giving them enough time to respond to a question or comment

- Accepts children's grammar without correcting

c) Supports the needs of dual language learners (when applicable - see pp. 109-115 for expanded examples)

- Is knowledgeable about and respectful of each child's family, cultural groups and home languages

- Establishes responsive and accepting relationships to help children feel confident to engage in receptive and verbal communication in either language (home language or new language)

6.5 Candidate promotes children's vocabulary development

a) Intentionally provides opportunities for children to learn new words

Examples

- Helps children learn subject-specific vocabulary (such as mathematics or science) by introducing terms such as *more than, less than, about, near, approximately and in between, etc.*

- Helps children connect word meaning(s) to experiences and real objects

- Explains words; uses synonyms and antonyms

Candidates seeking Bilingual Specialization must also show evidence of the following:

- Provides opportunities for all children to acquire a second language

- Helps children associate word meanings in both languages with familiar objects and experiences

- Takes an active role in labeling children's actions and surroundings in their home language, encouraging children's use of these words

b) Regularly introduces children to more advanced vocabulary

Examples

- Regularly introduces more complex vocabulary into conversations and Whole Group times

- Responds to children's speech with expansions and questions, introducing and explaining new words

- Does not correct children's grammatical speech errors. Instead, restates them correctly (For example, a child may say, "I gots two foots" and the teacher replies, "Yes, you have two feet so you need two socks.")

Functional Area 7: Creative

Candidate uses a variety of developmentally appropriate learning experiences and teaching strategies for children to explore music, movement and the visual arts and to develop and express their individual creative abilities.

Item 7.1 Activities and materials encourage children to express themselves through the visual arts.

Indicator:

a) **Art materials and activities are available for children daily**

Examples

- Open-ended drawing/coloring materials are available rather than coloring books/sheets

- Open-ended art activities are encouraged over product-oriented craft activities

- Activities that focus on processes are offered rather than activities intended only to create certain products

- Art activities, materials and techniques are offered that reflect the cultural groups of the classroom community

- Preschoolers are provided many colors of construction paper, water color markers; safety scissors, glue, glue sticks, stamp pads, tempera/watercolor paints, hole punches, collage materials, play dough or clay, chalk, paints, tapes, a variety of papers, brushes, found/recycled objects, or other art tools/materials

7.2 Activities and materials encourage children to dance, move and develop their musical abilities.

a) Music and dance/movement materials and activities are available for children daily

Examples

- Children do fingerplays, sing, dance and move creatively

- Children regularly hear a variety of musical forms and styles

- Children and adults make up songs and music together

- Children play with games with music/musical instruments

- Children are offered activities that explore rhythm

- Materials for free or organized play include musical sound toys, ribbons, scarves and musical instruments (such as drums, bells, triangles, wood blocks and tambourines)

- Music and dance activities are offered that reflect the cultural groups of the classroom community

7.3 Activities and materials encourage children to develop their imaginations.

a) Dramatic play materials and activities are available for children daily

Examples

- Activities include putting on plays, storytelling, puppetry, role-playing

- A variety of dress-up clothes are available (gender-specific and non-specific clothing, uniforms, costumes as well as clothing with large buttons, snaps, laces and zippers)

- A variety of dramatic play props (such as dolls, blankets, mirrors, purses, telephones, briefcases, a dollhouse, small people/animal figures; kitchen/office/restaurant/store props, puppets, puppet stage, etc.)

- Dramatic play activities and materials are offered that reflect the cultural groups of the classroom community

7.4 Candidate promotes individual expression and creativity.

a) Encourages creative self-expression in children's activities

Examples

- Keeps informed about cultural resources in the community and uses them with children when possible

- In the visual arts, children's "scribble" pictures are valued, their artwork is not expected to look like others

- In music & dance, children are encouraged to move in their own ways, make their own music and songs

- In dramatic play, encourages children to choose their own roles and create/use props in their own ways

- Participates in dramatic play to get it going if children have difficulty, or to extend it (such as, entering the play restaurant and pretending to be a customer, "Could I see a menu, please? I'd like to order dinner.")

- Helps children identify and imitate creative forms found in the art, music and dances of their cultural groups

- Models creativity (for example, displays her own artwork, reads children a poem she wrote or plays a guitar with children)

 Candidates seeking Bilingual Specialization must also show evidence of the following:

- Helps children express themselves creatively through activities in both languages

b) Facilitates child-directed and process-oriented creative experiences

Examples

- Plans activities that are not designed to result in identical finished products

- Allows children to create abstract art; does not expect children to always create representational products

- Does not present a model for a finished product

- Gradually introduces different art materials, giving children time to explore them in their own ways, showing interest in their process

- Encourages children to explore textures, colors and the sensory experiences of materials

- Offers the option to record children's descriptions of their work

- Encourages children by making positive, specific comments rather than empty praise (such as, "I see you mixed blue and yellow together," instead of "What a pretty painting")

- Asks open-ended questions such as "How did you make this pattern?"

- Encourages repeated exploration of creative materials over time (for example, letting a block structure stand so that building can continue the next day)

- In dramatic play, follows the child's lead, taking care not to over-stimulate or frighten the child

- Accepts/encourages flexible use of materials when possible (such as allowing children to carry pretend animals from the Science Area to the Sand Table or paint with a feather at an easel)

Competency Standard III:

To support social and emotional development and to provide positive guidance

Developmental Contexts

Self: Preschool children (3 through 5 years old) experience many conflicting feelings and ideas: independence and dependence, confidence and doubt, fear and power, hostility and love, anger and tenderness, and aggression and passivity. They continue to need a reliable environment and secure relationships with adults as they deal with these feelings and learn more about themselves in an expanding world: peers, school, neighborhood, and society. They are proud of their new skills in caring for themselves, developing friendships, building and making things work, understanding and achieving. Adults can support them by respecting and recognizing the strengths and needs of each child and by providing experiences that help them grow as individuals.

Social: Preschool children welcome social interactions with adults and children. Their social skills develop rapidly, first through parallel play, near other playing preschoolers, and gradually through more cooperative play, with them. Adults can promote understanding and respect among preschool children by providing experiences in sharing materials, responsibilities and social problem solving. Preschoolers can begin to learn about differing individual and group needs in a positive way.

Guidance: Preschool children can participate in the process of setting group rules and can benefit from learning why those rules are necessary. They require an understanding adult who remains calm and supportive as they continue to become self-regulated. They will continue to "test" limits from time to time as they grow more confident and independent. Adults can support them by acknowledging their feelings and remaining consistent about expectations, routines, and limits.

Functional Area 8: Self

Candidate develops a warm, positive, supportive and responsive relationship with each child and helps each child learn about and take pride in his or her individual and cultural identities.

Item 8.1 Children's environments support the development of positive self-concepts.

Indicator:

a) Spaces and activities help each child develop a sense of self-identity/worth

Examples

- Children have spaces to store their own things (such as cubbies/hooks/bins labeled with children's names and/or photos)

- Photos of children and families displayed throughout

- Children's works and names are displayed at their eye level

- Mirrors are hung at children's eye level

- Activities invite children to learn their names, addresses and the names of/ relationships with family members (such as games or songs about the children's names, creating family trees or albums, etc.)

- Books, pictures, stories and discussions help children identify with the events and experiences of their lives (for example, single-parent families, extended families, same-sex families, adoption, foster families, divorce, moving, birth of siblings, or death of family members or beloved pets).

- Indoor and outdoor environments are adapted so that children with special needs can maximize their independence

- All children, including those with special needs are provided activities that support them in feeling effective, experiencing success and gaining the positive recognition of others

b) Materials chosen provide children opportunities to experience success

Examples

- Materials selected provide developmentally appropriate challenges that each child can accomplish

- Over time, materials are changed to provide greater challenges as children develop

- Materials modified so that all children, including those with special needs, may experience success

8.2 Candidate's interactions help children develop positive self-concepts.

a) Respects the individuality of each child

Examples

- Knows and uses each child's preferred name

- Recognizes and respects each child's physical and emotional boundaries

- Gives one-on-one attention to each child as much as possible

- Talks to child about her/his family — where they are, when they will come back and what they will do together

- When appropriate, encourages and respects children's choices of play, materials and foods

- Encourages children to try new and different activities

- Allows children to move from one interest center to another rather than assigning them to specific centers

- Allows each child to work at her/his own pace and in his/her style

- Encourages children to choose any activity free of its traditionally gender-specific association

• Supports the individual independence of children with special needs, including them in physical and social activities with other children (making modifications when necessary)

• Able to speak some words in a child's home language (when applicable)

 Candidates seeking Bilingual Specialization must also show evidence of the following:

• Helps each child deal with stressors using the child's first language

b) Shows sensitivity to and acceptance of each child's feelings and needs

Examples

• Verbally recognizes a child's feelings

• Helps children to verbalize their feelings using storybook characters, puppets, dolls, etc.

• Helps children through periods of stress, separation, life transitions and other crises

• Welcomes a child who needs to be nurtured with a loving voice, hugging or appropriate physical contact

• Responds to children's feelings (such as love, joy, loneliness, anger or disappointment) with sympathetic/empathetic attention

• Quickly comforts children who are upset

• Helps children understand and appropriately express their own feelings

• Helps children recognize, accept and express feelings in culturally appropriate ways

• Respects children's preferences

• Is patient with each child

• Focuses on each child's positive qualities rather than comparing them with each other

• Celebrates children's cultural identities

• Promotes cooperation over competition

- Does not criticize children's efforts

- Understands the effect of abuse and neglect on children's self-concept and works sensitively with such children

8.3 Candidate encourages children to develop a sense of independence.

a) Encourages children's self-help/ self-regulation skills while being respectful of family preferences and cultural differences

Examples

- Encourages preschoolers to clean up their own spills

- Helps children learn to share and wait turns

- Encourages children to write their names

- Supports children's efforts to dress themselves

- Encourages children to serve themselves foods and drinks

b) Ensures that toileting is a developmentally appropriate, positive experience for children

Examples

- Encourages toilet learning when each child is ready and interested

- Does not shame or rush children

- Shows children how to use good toilet habits (such as wiping properly, lifting and lowering seat and aiming well)

- Encourages children to use the toilet by themselves

- Does not reward or punish children for toileting behaviors

c) Promotes each child's growing sense of autonomy

Examples

- Asks children to push in their chairs

- Encourages children to clean up after themselves

- Encourages children to clear their own places when ready

- Teaches appropriate table behaviors

- Invites children to participate in simple food preparation

- Asks children to set table

- Demonstrates for children how to use certain materials or equipment that might be challenging (such as how to climb a ladder or hammer a nail)

Functional Area 9: Social

Candidate helps each child function effectively in the group, learn to express feelings, acquire social skills and make friends. Candidate promotes mutual respect among children and adults.

Item 9.1 The classroom environment provides opportunities for children to experience cooperation.

Indicator:

a) **Materials, equipment and activities provided help children experience working and playing in harmony**

Examples

- Some manipulatives, materials or equipment require cooperation between children

- Children participate in some activities in small groups

- Some games provided invite teamwork

- Children are asked to cooperate when serving or passing foods during snack/meal times

- Children hold hands with partner when walking in hall or outside

9.2 A non-biased environment is provided.

a) **Diverse activities, materials, curricula and/or events reflect multiple cultural groups, ethnicities and family structures**

Examples

- Pictures, posters, books, and other materials reflect and celebrate diversity in cultural groups, ages, genders, differing abilities and varied family structures

- Languages, real objects, music, art, foods and many aspects of cultural groups are incorporated into the curriculum

- Props associated with special needs and diverse cultural groups are included in Dramatic Play and throughout the classroom

- Holidays/events are celebrated that reflect the diverse families of the classroom community

- Members of the local community are invited to share aspects their lives (such as hobbies, cooking, talents, holidays, dress, etc.) with the children

 Candidates seeking Bilingual Specialization must also show evidence of the following:

- Uses objects, music activities and celebrations that are meaningful to young children to encourage development of both languages and cultural groups

9.3 Candidate promotes children's sense of belonging in the classroom community.

a) Encourages children's social interactions

Examples

- Provides many opportunities for children to collaborate, interact and play with each other

- Helps children learn to respect the rights and possessions of others

- Encourages children to comfort and help one another

- Acknowledges children's caring or helpful behaviors

- Understands that the social roles and expectations for children in their family setting may be different from those of the child care program, helping the children successfully socialize in both settings

- Encourages children to make friends by modeling friendly behavior with other children and adults

- Encourages children to interact with each other in playful and caring ways

- Acknowledges and encourages children's positive behaviors toward one another

- Helps children, including those shy and aggressive, to get along with others

- Ensures positive integration of all children including those with special needs (when applicable)

- Acknowledges when children assert their rights in socially acceptable ways

- Creates opportunities for social interactions between children, facilitating as necessary

- Encourages cooperation rather than competition

- Encourages and supports children to make friends, especially those who are isolated from or rejected by peers

- Encourages children to ask for, accept, and give help to one another

- Encourages children to work together in maintaining their environments (such as repairing broken books/toys, cleaning up materials, keeping playgrounds litter-free, etc.)

 Candidates seeking Bilingual Specialization must also show evidence of the following:

- Understands that the social roles and expectations for bilingual children in their family setting may be different from those of the child care program, helping the children successfully socialize in both settings

- Encourages children who are fluent in either language to help less fluent children

b) Models appropriate social interactions

Examples

- Models effective social skills by building a positive relationship with each child, parent and other adults in the center

- Models social skills by engaging in social interactions with children (such as conversing with children at mealtime or while putting toys away)

- Warmly introduces newcomers

- Models for and teaches children skills that help them learn how to join in, start and sustain play with other children

- Models and participates in dialogues or conversations with children

9.4 Candidate helps children experience sympathy/empathy and respect for others.

a) Helps children understand their feelings and the feelings of others

Examples

- Helps children recognize their own and others' feelings, similarities and differences in order to help them begin learning how to empathize with others

- Talks with a child about another child's feelings

- Labels children's feelings and the feelings of others (such as "George seems sad because his mommy left. Do you remember how you felt when your mom left this morning?")

- Acknowledges children's developing empathetic responses to one another and adults

- Encourages children to express how they feel

- Models empathy

- Helps children to see how what they do affects others

b) Discusses diversity comfortably when interacting with children

Examples

- Discusses comfortably with children the subjects of family, ethnic, cultural, gender or social groups

- Uses children's individual differences as opportunities for learning about how people are alike and different

- Helps children recognize and appreciate racial, ethnic and ability differences and similarities

- Understands children's curiosities about their own and others' bodies, responding with developmentally appropriate information (such as explaining the physical differences between boys and girls matter-of-factly, in simple terms)

- Encourages children to share stories and activities from their families and cultural groups

- Encourages play and relationships among all children across racial, language, ethnic, age, and gender groupings, including children with special needs

- Models equitable treatment of all children and families

Functional Area 10: Guidance

Candidate provides a supportive environment and uses effective strategies to support children's self-regulation and acceptable behaviors. Candidate effectively intervenes for children with persistent, challenging behaviors.

Item 10.1 Spaces and materials are arranged to promote positive interactions and limit disruptive behaviors.

Indicator:

a) Spaces and materials provided anticipate children's behavioral and developmental needs

Examples

- Ample space provided for groups of children to move and play

- Equipment is available for children who need to move

- Multiple copies of popular toys are provided to minimize conflicts and waiting

- Furniture is arranged to reduce running

- Space that feels private (but is well-supervised) is provided for children who need time to be alone

- New materials are introduced/explained at Circle Time before children use them

10.2 Candidate proactively implements methods for preventing behavioral problems.

a) Acknowledges positive behaviors

Examples

- Verbally or non-verbally acknowledges children's self-regulation and kind behavior

- Ignores minor distractions

- Comments directly, sincerely, and positively to children about their performance and ideas

- Uses methods that support the development of internal motivation rather than stickers or other rewards

b) Models appropriate behaviors

Examples

- Models sharing, taking turns, waiting

- Models social problem-solving (how to resolve a conflict with someone else)

- Models appropriate ways for children to behave (such as using an "inside" voice)

c) Provides firm, consistent limits and expectations

Examples

- Helps children understand that kind, cooperative behavior is expected

- Gives positively worded directions (such as "Give gentle touches" rather than "Don't hit")

- Involves children in the creation of Classroom Rules

- Explains the reasons for rules in clear language, demonstrating whenever possible

- Allows children to figure out their own solutions, providing support as needed

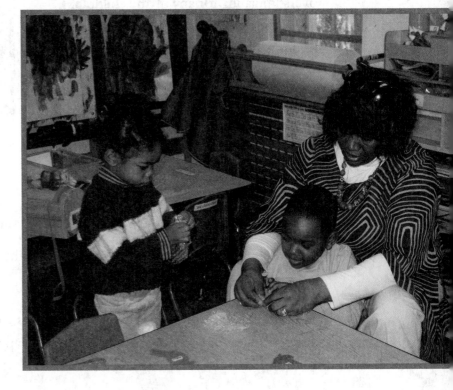

Candidates seeking Bilingual Specialization must also show evidence of the following:

• Uses clear and simple words in both languages to describe limits and expectations

d) Uses effective classroom management techniques

Examples

• Is aware of each child's limitations, temperament, developmental levels, cultural groups, etc. and individualizes guidance accordingly

• Moves about room as children play, talking with and helping them, encouraging children to participate

• Explains rules at the child's level of understanding and/or includes children in creating rules

• Gives children acceptable choices when appropriate and follows what each child chooses (for example, "Do you want to read a book with me or play on the climber?" or "Should we have apples or bananas for snack today?")

• Is able to modify play when it becomes overstimulating for any of the children, including children with disabilities or sensitive temperaments

• Anticipates confrontations between children and defuses provocative behaviors

• Makes sure there is enough room at the table or play area so children are not crowded

• Reinforces positive behaviors

• Anticipates and prevents the escalation of confrontations between children.

• Addresses the problem behavior or situation rather than labeling the child involved

• Explains the reasons for limits in simple words, demonstrating whenever possible

• Anticipates and responds to children's behaviors, knowing each child's individual differences/tendencies to bite, pinch, climb, escape, etc.

e) Helps children learn to articulate their emotions and practice how to respond in challenging situations

Examples

- Helps children use words rather than actions to resolve conflicts

- Supports children in finding alternate behaviors that meet their needs when undesirable but developmentally expected social behaviors occur (such as biting, hitting, spitting, etc.)

- Accepts and helps children accept "negative" feelings and find safe ways to deal with them

- Provides activities such as throwing foam balls, bean bags, manipulating playdough to children who need to release negative feelings peacefully

10.3 Candidate uses positive techniques when reacting to children's challenging behaviors.

a) Places emphasis on the development of self-discipline/self-regulation

Examples

- Uses gentle reminders when rules are momentarily forgotten or not followed

- Teaches children positive alternatives to socially unacceptable behavior (such as teaching a child to "use your words" rather than grabbing a toy from another child)

b) Deals with challenging behaviors in a consistent and calm manner

Examples

- Assesses challenging behaviors or conflicts as they arise, intervening when appropriate

- Uses a range of effective strategies to individualize each child's guidance

- Responds consistently over time to each child's behavioral problems

- Responds quickly and calmly to prevent children from hurting each other

- Is fair and firm if "no" must be said

- Avoids power struggles

- Maintains calm self-control when dealing with an aggressive child

- Communicates with children effectively when behavioral issues arise (such as positioning herself at their eye level, speaking softly/privately, using positive but serious facial expressions/body language, etc.)

c) Uses appropriate techniques to address negative behaviors

Examples

- Uses redirection, providing children with a variety of positive options, stating clearly what children can do

- Uses normal social consequences to teach cause and effect (for example, if a child leaves a cap off a marker, Candidate lets marker dry out, later drawing child's attention to the result)

- Facilitates conflict resolution processes (such as acting as a mediator to help children solve problems, listening and asking open-ended questions to get children to think through solutions)

- Facilitates creative problem-solving, eliciting multiple ideas from children for solutions to problems

- Provides children time and space to solve their own problems whenever possible

- Uses firm "no" only when necessary to maintain children's safety, moving the child or dangerous object, giving a simple explanation (for example, "It is not safe for you to climb on the table. I don't want you to fall and get hurt.")

- When responding to tantrums, isolates and stays close to the child when she/he may hurt or do damage, letting the other children know that "she is having a difficult moment and I am helping her stay safe."

- Does not use negative disciplinary methods (such as spanking, threatening, shouting, isolating, shaming or time-outs)

Competency Standard IV:

To establish positive and productive relationships with families

Developmental Context

Families: Preschool children (3 through 5 years old) move back and forth from their family to the child care program more independently than younger children. They are also more sensitive to the differences between the two environments and observe carefully the interactions between their parents and teachers/caregivers. Teachers/caregivers should build a "partnership" with each family to best support the needs of each child. They should keep each other informed of important developments in children's lives and provide mutual support in nurturing each child's physical, social, emotional and cognitive development.

Functional Area 11: Families

Candidate establishes a positive, responsive, cooperative relationship with each child's family, engages in two-way communication with families, encourages their involvement in the program and supports the child's relationship with her/his family.

Item 11.1 Various opportunities to appreciate and communicate with children's families are included as part of the regular program.

Indicator:

a) **Room displays and materials reflect respect for various communities, cultural groups and families**

Examples

- Photos/posters of diverse children and their families are displayed at children's eye level

- Books/albums with pictures of children, their families and their communities are accessible to children

- "Family Trees" are displayed that provide images of the families in the classroom community

 Candidates seeking Bilingual Specialization must also show evidence of the following:

- Environment clearly communicates to the families that their home language is valued and respected

b) Opportunities to communicate with and distribute information to families are provided

Examples

- Family Board ensures that families have access to current information about the program

- Each child/family has a designated container for classroom or program "mail," artwork, writing samples, etc. (such as pouches, folders, bins)

- Regular (daily, weekly) communications are sent home that provide families with information about current/upcoming events, classroom needs, etc. (such as newsletters, blogs, emails, texts or through a regularly-updated website)

11.2 Candidate appreciates the uniqueness of each family.

a) Welcomes and respects every family

Examples

- Knows family members and greets them by name

- Appropriately uses information about each child's family in conversations, program activities, conferences and throughout the curriculum

- Recognizes that parents and family are the most important people in children's lives, making sure to never create a sense of competition

- Welcomes and encourages family members to visit throughout the day

- Helps parents with separations from child, recognizing parents' possible concerns about leaving their child

- Invites families to take part in program activities

- Honors each family's dietary, dress or other preferences for their children

- Respects each family's cultural background, religious beliefs, and childrearing practices, negotiating openly any areas of discomfort or concern

- Respects families' views when they differ from the program's goals or policies and attempts to resolve the differences

- Recognizes that children's primary caregivers may be single mothers or fathers, two parents of the same or different genders, stepparents, grandparents, uncles, aunts, sisters, brothers, foster parents, or guardians

 Candidates seeking Bilingual Specialization must also show evidence of the following:

- Greets visitors using salutations in both languages

11.3 Candidate partners with families to support the needs of their children.

a) Works closely with each family

Examples

- Encourages families to share their views about childrearing, guidance and self-regulation

- Builds a trusting relationship with children and families

- Develops close relationships with children that do not compete with their family relationships

- Helps families understand their child's temperament, providing and soliciting further ideas and suggestions for support

- Supports and encourages families in becoming observers of their children

- Helps families cope with and plan for supportive transitions into and out of the program as well as from room to room.

- Gives families an integral role in establishing goals for their children's learning and development

- Encourages and assists parents to communicate confidently about their children with government and other community agencies

- Collaborates with families to plan program events and topics for discussion

b) Maintains open communication with families

Examples

- Communicates frequently with parents about children's health, nutrition, communicable diseases and medications

- Sends home written observations and explanations of what children learned, experienced and achieved

- Encourages families to share observations, anecdotes and perspectives about their child

- Is able to discuss learning challenges or problem behaviors with families in a constructive, supportive manner

- Shares with families her/his pleasure in each child's new abilities

- Shares children's achievements with parents (such as communication/language, physical, social, cognitive, etc.)

- Discusses problem behaviors with families in a strengths-based, constructive, supportive manner

- Regularly holds conferences during which teachers and families can share information about children's progress at home and in the program.

- Conducts home visits or if parents prefer, meets privately with them at a comfortable site (such as a library or local community center)

- Shows sincere interest in what families share and exchanges information regularly with parents about the child's life at home and in the center, including routines and changes in care, favorite activities, upcoming developmental expectations, etc.

- Provides oral and written communication with parents in their preferred language

- Respects the language of non-English-speaking families, encouraging them to communicate freely with their children in their preferred language and helping them find opportunities to learn English

Candidates seeking Bilingual Specialization must also show evidence of the following:

- Regularly communicates orally and in writing with parents and children in their preferred language

- Provides written information for families in both languages (such as classroom newsletters, notices about immunizations, program policies, notices of upcoming events, etc.)

11.4 Candidate helps families understand and support the healthy growth and development of their child.

a) Provides information and opportunities to help families meet their child's developmental needs

Examples

- Helps families understand the importance of play for children

- Helps families understand the importance of creative expression and the need to provide children with opportunities for creative activities such as storytelling, playing make-believe, using art materials, etc.

- Works with parents to address issues of obesity and shares appropriate literature

- Sends home articles, brochures on various topics related to child development

- Offers a parent resource library of books, magazines, journals, dvds, etc.

- Provides a website with links to various parenting and child development resources

- Empathizes with families around stressful areas of parenting, such as lack of sleep, illnesses, challenging behaviors, providing support and suggestions for strategies when asked

- Shares realistic expectations with families about children's behaviors in ways that help avoid disciplinary problems (for example, discussing how long children can sit still or that young children cannot yet follow multiple step directions).

- Provides parent education events with local speakers

- Invites parents to observe the children and discuss their observations

- Helps parents recognize their feelings and attitudes about special needs

 Candidates seeking Bilingual Specialization must also show evidence of the following:

- Understands the principles and characteristics of bilingual language development in children and explains these to parents

- Helps families understand the importance of children learning their primary language and cultural group

- Helps families understand the program goals for bilingual development

- Explains to families in their second language safety practices used in the classroom

- Regularly communicates with parents about their child's bilingual development and helps them find ways to support this within the family

- Supports families' desire to communicate their language and cultural heritage to their children

- If using translated material, ensures the information is as relevant and accurate as the original provided in English

b) Knows the social service, health and education resources of the community, engaging them when appropriate

Examples

- Helps families find resources about possible impairments or delays that affect hearing and speech

- Observes and evaluates children's physical development, recognizing signs of possible physical disabilities and developmental delays, referring parents to appropriate services, and following up on referrals or individual development plans

- Recognizes that sometimes serious behavior problems are related to developmental or emotional problems and works cooperatively with parents and other professionals towards solutions

- Works with family members and specialists to develop plans specific to the needs of each child and works with the family to meet goals for the child

- Establishes relationships (through a liaison) with community services that respond to family violence (such as Parents Anonymous, Child Protective Services and local shelter programs)

- Works as part of a team to help identify, diagnose, and implement individualized plans for children with special needs

- Shares with families clear and understandable information about their children's special needs and information about the family's legal right to services

- Informs families about resources (such as physicians or community clinics) which provide services to families in their primary language

- Provides information about local language translation services, as needed

 Candidates seeking Bilingual Specialization must also show evidence of the following:

- Informs families about resources (such as physicians or community clinics) which provide services to families in their primary language

- Helps parents identify resources in their homes, families, and community that will support the development of both languages

c) Recommends activities families can do at home that support their child's development

Examples

- Helps families find ways to play and learn with their children (such as sending home activity bags, storybooks, manipulatives, art materials, etc.)

- Suggests experiences and inexpensive/common materials that can support play and learning at home

- Shares ideas with parents about the learning opportunities for children in everyday household tasks and routines

Competency Standard V:

To ensure a well-run, purposeful program that is responsive to participant needs

Functional Area 12: Program Management

Candidate uses observation, documentation and planning to support children's development and learning and to ensure effective operation of the classroom or group. Candidate is a competent organizer, record keeper, communicator and cooperative co-worker.

Item 12.1 Candidate observes, documents and assesses each child's developmental/educational progress.

Indicator:

a) **Objectively observes and records information about children's behaviors and learning**

Examples

- Regularly observes each child's developmental/educational progress

- When observing/documenting, only records behavioral facts (objective statements rather than assumptions or subjective biases that could lead to misinterpretations (such as "Vincent smiled" rather than "Vincent was happy" or "Liana threw a block which knocked over Brandy's block castle" rather than "Liana wanted to knock over Brandy's block castle"

• Collects observational examples to support concerns regarding potential learning or behavioral needs or abilities

b) Analyzes and assesses multiple sources of evidence in order to set appropriate developmental goals for each child/group, planning curriculum accordingly

Examples

• Uses multiple sources of evidence when assessing the strengths, interests, abilities, and needs of each child (such as written observations, information from parents, data from formal and informal observation tools, individual portfolios, work samples, etc.)

• Considers the cultural expectations of each child when interpreting observations and setting goals

• Reflects on previous experiences in order to make intentional choices when planning curricula

• Uses Individualized Education Programs (IEPs) to inform curriculum planning for children, when applicable

• Accesses resources such as state early learning guidelines, when available, as a guide for planning

 Candidates seeking Bilingual Specialization must also show evidence of the following:

• Makes use of available evaluation instruments in the second language

12.2 Candidate adheres to regulatory requirements and program policies.

a) Adheres to current local child care regulations and program policies

Examples

• Abides by all legal and program requirements

• Adheres to group size requirements

• Complies with teacher-child ratio requirements

• Can articulate the philosophy, goals and objectives of the program to others

b) Adheres to professional Mandated Reporting requirements related to abuse and neglect

Examples

- Recognizes symptoms of possible abuse and neglect and

- Is alert to play or behavior that indicates physical or sexual abuse

- Seeks out resources for information and support if physical, emotional or sexual abuse is suspected, following state law in response

- Responds sensitively to child's and family's needs, collaborating in carrying out treatment plans

c) Maintains current records on children's health, safety and behavior

Examples

- Keeps up-to-date records (such as attendance, accident/incident reports, child health and emergency forms, etc.) as required by regulations or policies, sharing the information with parents, specialists and other center personnel, only when appropriate

- Retains parents' written authorizations of all persons allowed to pick up children from the program

12.3 Candidate maintains effective professional relationships.

a) Establishes cooperative interpersonal relationships with coworkers, colleagues, volunteers and supervisors

Examples

- Supports other staff by offering assistance and support when needed

- Works as a member of a team with others in the classroom and the program, including substitutes, parents and volunteers

- Coordinates program plans with parents, specialists and program personnel, when appropriate

- Maintains professional relationship with supervisors

- Accepts supervision in the performance of duties

- Participates in peer evaluation and is able to accept comments and criticism from colleagues, supervisors and parents in a constructive way

Competency Standard VI:

To maintain a commitment to professionalism

Functional Area 13: Professionalism

Candidate makes decisions based on knowledge of research-based early childhood practices, promotes high-quality in child care services and takes advantage of opportunities to improve knowledge and competence, both for personal and professional growth and for the benefit of children and families.

Item 13.1 Candidate commits to highest standards for professional practices.

Indicator:

a) **Protects the confidentiality of information about children, their families and the child care program**

   Examples

   • Discusses sensitive issues with discretion, only with appropriate staff, following up on their resolution

   • Observes strict confidentiality regarding the private issues of children and families, except as required by laws for reporting child abuse and neglect

   • Informs parents of confidentiality policy

b) **Conducts her/himself in a professional manner at all times**

   Examples

   • Demonstrates a clear understanding of job expectations

   • Has a positive attitude and work ethic, maintaining energy and enthusiasm

   • Arrives at work on time every day

   • Dresses appropriately for the responsibilities of the position

   • Displays good judgment when making decisions that affect the children in her/his care

13.2 Candidate works with other professionals and families to communicate the needs of children and families to decision makers.

a) Advocates for the needs of children and families

Examples

- Advocates for additional resources for individual children or some aspect of the program

- Promotes high quality services for children and families

- Stands for the rights of children and families in public forums

 Candidates seeking Bilingual Specialization must also show evidence of the following:

- Promotes the effective functioning of the bilingual program by attempting to clarify issues relating to bilingualism and multiculturalism

- Advocates for the needs of children and families who speak a different language and operate in a different cultural context

13.3 Candidate takes advantage of opportunities to continue professional growth.

a) Learns about new laws and regulations affecting child care, children, and families

Examples

- Keeps informed about child care practices, research, legislation and other developments in the field of early care and learning using a variety of methods, including online opportunities and digital media

- Keeps abreast of proposed regulatory, legislative and workforce issues that affect the welfare of young children and families

- Seeks information about laws/policies and support strategies for children and families child affected by physical/sexual abuse and neglect

b) Takes opportunities for professional and personal development by reflecting, joining professional organizations and attending meetings, training courses and conferences

Examples

- Is a "life-long learner," continuing to gain knowledge about child development and early childhood best practices

- Regularly reflects on own performance to identify needs for professional growth

- Maintains an active membership in an early childhood association(s)

- Seeks information relevant to the needs of the children in her/his care from professional resources (such as journals, community college courses, workshops, online websites/trainings, etc.)

- Participates in Professional Learning Communities with colleagues and community members

- Seeks feedback from a trusted mentor or coach

- Continues to increase knowledge about child development in order to help children and parents deal with typical developmental issues (such as separation anxiety, crying, dependency, willfulness, challenging behaviors, shyness, sexual identity and making friends)

- Increases knowledge about dual language learning and inclusion by reading, attending workshops and consulting professionals

 Candidates seeking Bilingual Specialization must also show evidence of the following:

- Stays informed about the latest developments in bilingual education by reading articles, attending workshops and consulting with professionals

- Maintains and works to increase fluency in her/his second language

Note:

Also included in the CDA Comprehensive Scoring Instrument at the back of this book, as an indicator of her/his professionalism, is **Item 13.4**, the Candidate's completion of the required Professional Portfolio during the CDA credentialing process.

Part3

Additional Information & Resources

- Overseas Assessments
- ADA Accommodations
- Principles for Dual Language Learners
- CDA Professional Development (PD) Specialist™ Eligibility Requirements
- The CDA Verification Visit® Reflective Dialogue
- CDA® Exam Question Examples
- Glossary
- Application
- Forms
- Comprehensive Scoring Instrument

Overseas Assessments

The Council currently conducts CDA assessments only in the United States, Puerto Rico and in the overseas installations of the U.S. Military Child Development Services of all Military Branches. If Candidates outside the United States or Puerto Rico want to obtain the CDA Credential, they must contact the Council to discuss any special protocols and additional expenses.

ADA Accommodations

The Council for Professional Recognition's mission is to provide the opportunity for all early childhood education professionals to participate in a fair and standardized CDA assessment process to demonstrate their competence and knowledge.

The CDA credentialing process is in full compliance with ADA requirements. The Council will provide reasonable accommodations to all eligible Candidates who provide the proper medical documentation.

For more information, please contact the Council *before you apply* at 800-424-4310 to discuss any special arrangements that may need to be made for your CDA Verification Visit® and CDA Exam.

Principles for Dual Language Learners

Young children whose home language is not English are participants in many early childhood centers and family child care homes. These children are referred to as dual language learners because they are either learning two languages simultaneously or adding a new (second) language to their primary (home) language. The following developmental principles and accompanying practice examples are presented separately to emphasize that they apply to all Competency Standards and Functional Areas. These principles and examples provide important guidance to help teachers work competently with dual language learners.

Developmental Context

Infants and toddlers exposed to two languages at home or in an early childhood program have the opportunity to develop basic language ability in two languages simultaneously (simultaneous dual-language acquisition). However, when young children (aged 3, 4 and 5 years) whose families' primary language is not English begin participating in a preschool or family child care home, they have most likely established basic language ability in their home language. For these children this opportunity for second language acquisition is referred to as sequential dual-language acquisition. Early childhood programs can also offer opportunities for second language acquisition to children whose home language is English. However, the following developmental principles and examples focus on young English language learners in preschool programs.

The research literature on second language acquisition identifies the following four developmental stages (Tabors, 2008; Espinosa, 2010):

1. Home language use

Young children who have established basic oral communication ability in their home language naturally enter the preschool setting using their familiar home language. The degree to which these children experience being understood by others depends on whether any of the adults or children speak their home language.

2. Nonverbal/observational period

When young children speaking their home language are frequently not understood, they begin speaking less and turn their attention to observing, listening and using and nonverbal means of communication. This developmental stage is very important as the child is actively learning the sounds, words, and rules of the new language. These children are building their receptive understanding of their new language — connecting the sounds and words to people, objects, and experiences. There can be wide variance in the amount of time any child operates at this stage of development.

3. Telegraphic and formulaic speech

Children begin trying out their new language, using simple words or phrases to express thoughts, requests, and directions. Although the child may not know the specific meaning of these words and phrases, dual language learners are focused on results — do they work for social interactions or achieve the desired response from an adult. This form of early language production also enables these children to begin participating in group singing or reciting rhymes.

4. Productive language

Dual language learners begin building their own original sentences using words and phrases they have been hearing and practicing. This is a gradual phase as children test what works and experiment with applying grammar rules of their new language. Each child's productive language is closely related to their expansion of receptive language.

Adults who successfully work with young dual language learners understand that although each of the above developmental stages build on each other, beginning to use productive language does not replace earlier phases in particular situations. In some circumstances a child will revert to nonverbal observation and listening. Effective teachers are also sensitive to numerous factors that influence the rate and proficiency of each child's acquisition of a new language — amount and quality of exposure to English; age and culture; motivation and interest in new language; personality; and degree of accepting relationships that support trying new language (Tabors, 2008). Understanding that there will be individual differences between children is essential to providing the best possible support for dual language development.

An extremely important component of good early childhood programs and family child care homes is providing a learning environment that is supportive of the language development of all children. For dual language learners this means providing age appropriate, individually appropriate, and culturally appropriate experiences that help children begin to understand and use the English language while simultaneously developing their primary (home) language. This includes encouraging parents to provide their children with a strong foundation in their home language.

When a child's second language (typically English) is used predominantly by the surrounding society, home language development and maintenance may become more difficult. Nevertheless, research shows that second language learners do best in school when they have a strong grounding in their home language (Espinosa, 2010; Oiler & Eilers, 2002; Slavin & Cheung, 2005). The loss of the first language can be detrimental not only for personal, familial, religious, and cultural reasons, but it can also negatively impact children's progress in school. Teachers can help families value and support their child to continue developing the home language while also learning a second language.

Indicators of Competence with Dual Language Learners

a) **The competent Candidate working with dual language learners is knowledgeable about and respectful of child's family, culture, and home language.**

Examples

- Seeks information about language spoken at home and child's proficiency in the home language.

- Expresses interest in, and respects, families' priorities related to their child including attitude toward maintaining home language and acquiring English.

- Makes effort to learn about child's home culture and beliefs as well as the people, pets, activities and objects that are familiar and important to the child. Incorporates appropriate artifacts and pictures into the center to help introduce English words and phrases for things already familiar to the preschooler.

- Maintains communication with families and/or child's primary caregiver to track the child's developmental gains in the home language.

- Is knowledgeable about and respectful of child's family.

- Asks parents for a few words in the home language that can be used to welcome the child in the classroom (*e.g., with parents' permission makes a tape recording of these words to use in the classroom to comfort their child and to help other children hear the sounds of the child's home language*).

b) **The competent Candidate working with dual language learners establishes responsive and accepting relationships to help children feel confident to engage in receptive and verbal communication in either language — home language or new language.**

Examples

- Builds positive, warm, nurturing relationships with dual language learners so that they feel safe and less anxious. Speaks English in ways that help dual language learners understand: uses simple sentences, repeats what is said, uses gestures and facial expressions, points to objects, uses everyday vocabulary.

- Speaks English clearly and slowly but not loudly, simplifying language when needed as you would for a younger child who is just learning their first language so the child more easily hears and learns individual words and phrases.

- Uses repetition so child hears the same word or phrase multiple times and consistently paired with the same object, person, or action.

- Gradually complicates own language so dual language learners continue to make progress in vocabulary development.

- Individualizes interactions that help each child gain trust in new people and environment.

- Is responsive and encouraging when child attempts verbal communication in either language — home language or new language.

- Provides verbal respectful response in the language the child is attempting to speak *(if possible)*.

- Recognizes when child mouths words or says words to self and encourages these attempts.

- Provides social support for dual language learners — regular contact with other children or adults who speak their language to help support their identity and help them make sense of what's going on.

- Provides lots of time and opportunities for children to play and talk among themselves.

- Encourages interactions between dual-language learners and English-speaking children by modeling initiations *(e.g., Candidate says to a child "Ask Lili, may I play with you?")*.

- Pairs an English language learner with an outgoing English-speaking child for certain periods during the day, so that the English-speaking child may help to integrate the English language learner into classroom activities.

c) **The competent Candidate working with dual language learners provides numerous appropriate experiences to help children gain receptive understanding of the new language — specifically, to hear the sounds of the new language and connect them to people, objects and experiences.**

Examples

- Uses predictable, comfortable classroom routines so dual language learners know what to expect and uses consistent language when referring to activities *(clean up time)* and objects *(cubby, house area, block area, monkey bars, etc.)* throughout the day in the classroom and outdoors.

- Provides pictures to accompany the daily schedule, classroom rules, and other print in the classroom to help children know the expectations even though they may not yet understand the language.

- Consistently accompanies verbal communications with gestures, actions, visual aids, or directed gaze to help child interpret directions *(e.g. models washing hands while saying "Let's wash your hands")* or descriptions of actions *(e.g. "Here is your jacket, or book, or snack")*.

- Helps children link English vocabulary to firsthand experiences with pictures, concrete objects and real-life events. For the most part, talks about the here and now, until children become more proficient in English.

- Selects books, songs and poems with repetitive language and repeats them frequently. Uses music and physical actions to help children learn new phrases and sentences *("Head, shoulders, knees, and toes")*.

- Reads books, if possible in child's primary language prior to reading the book in English, always pointing to pictures associated with words and phrases.

- Provides small group reading times using concept books or predictable texts *(like Brown Bear, Brown Bear)* with simplified vocabulary where children can clearly see the pictures and follow along. Reads the same book repeatedly, as long as children are enjoying it, to build comprehension. Reads *(or provides audiotapes)* in the child's home language.

- Describes in simple words and phrases the actions of the child *(e.g., "You are rolling the ball")* or actions of other children he/she is observing *(e.g., "Molly is rocking the doll")*.

- Places words at the end of the sentence to give emphasis to those words *(e.g. "You have red shoes. Billy has black shoes")*.

- Keeps alert to a dual language learner's use of non-verbal communication, such as pointing silently to a milk carton. Supplies the words in English for what the child is trying to convey *(e.g., "would you like more milk? Sure, I will be glad to give you more milk.")*

- Intentionally introduces new vocabulary words and uses the words throughout the day.

d) The competent Candidate working with dual language learners provides experiences to encourage and help children practice sounds and words of the new

language taking into account the stages and patterns of home language and English acquisition as well as information about each child's progress in cognitive, social-emotional, and physical development.

Examples

- Encourages child to repeat words as she or he demonstrates what objects or pictures they refer to.

- Gives child lots of time to think about what they want to say and waits to offer options of the word or phrase they are searching for when the child appears to wish for help.

- Asks young learners of the second language close-ended questions and offers some options for their response *(e.g., "Do you want the doll or do you want the clown?").*

- Pauses and lets the child fill in the next word when reading books.

- Provides opportunities to be able to answer in chorus with all the children.

- Helps children go from non-verbal responses to more expressive responses *(e.g., child looks at his shirt with spilled juice and looks at the Candidate; Candidate responds "Do you need me to change your shirt?" Child: "change shirt." Candidate: "That is right, I will be glad to change your shirt.")*

- Is able to expand child's vocabulary *(e.g., child says "yucky." Candidate responds "Yes, the floor is really dirty, yucky").*

- Notices words or phrases the child says *("me", "like", "more")* and helps child build from those words or phrases *(Candidate says "I like you!" "You want more").*

- Provides experiences for the child to play with the sounds: lullabies, repetitive singing and games, poems that repeat words.

- Understands that code switching or language mixing are typical and natural aspects of second language acquisition and enhances communication, and does not impose rigid rules about language *(e.g., child says "me asustado del doggie." Candidate responds: "Oh, I know — you are afraid of dogs").*

- Models correct English version of a phrase used by a dual language learner *(e.g., if a child says "I goed to park," the Candidate responds: "You went to the park? Who went with you?")*

- Engages child in conversations of topics that are interesting and important to him/her and that are part of their life experience

- Provides English language learners opportunities for one-on-one interaction with another child or adult where they may be more comfortable trying out English. But also plans for English language learners to have small group experiences — sometimes with children who are English language learners and other times with mixed groups of English speaking and English language learning children because each context offers different growth opportunities.

- Helps children acquire skills, knowledge, and attitudes such as book knowledge and appreciation, print awareness, letter knowledge, and phonological awareness in their home language. Once acquired, these skills will transfer as children become proficient in English.

- Includes environmental print *(signs, labels, books, magazines, newspapers and other text)* in English and the child's home language.

References:

Espinosa, L. (2010). *Getting it right for young children from diverse backgrounds: Applying research to improve practice.* Upper Saddle River, NJ: Pearson.

Oller, K. D., & Eilers, R. E. (Eds.). (2002). *Language and literacy in bilingual children.* New York: Multi-Lingual Matters.

Slavin, R. E., & Cheung, A. (2005). A synthesis of research on language of reading instruction for English language learners. *Review of Educational Research,* 75 (2), 247-281.

Tabors, P.O. (2008). *One child, two languages: A guide for early childhood educators of children learning English as a second language (2nd ed.).* Baltimore: Paul H. Brookes Publishing, Co.

CDA Professional Development (PD) Specialist™ Eligibility Requirements

To conduct CDA Verification Visits® as a CDA PD Specialist™, an individual must meet the following criteria:

Technology

- Must have a valid email address

- Must have access to the Internet

Personal

- Must be able to relate to people of various racial, ethnic, and socio-economic backgrounds

- Must be knowledgeable about local, state, and national requirements and standards for child care programs serving children aged birth through 5 years

- Must be able to conduct CDA Verification Visits during normal operating hours of early childhood programs

- PD Specialists conducting bilingual CDA Verification Visits must be bilingual

- PD Specialists conducting monolingual CDA Verification Visits must speak the language of the Monolingual Specialization

Education

- Must hold a Baccalaureate or Associate degree from an accredited college or university in one of the following disciplines:

  - Early Childhood Education/Child Development

  - Elementary Education/Early Childhood Education

  - Home Economics/Child Development

- The degree must include, at minimum, 18 semester or 24 quarter hours of coursework in Early Childhood Education/Child Development, focused on children birth through 5 years

Experience

Option 1:

For those with a Baccalaureate degree or higher, two years in a child care setting serving children from birth to 5 years of age to include:

- One year working directly with children as a caregiver, teacher, child life worker, social worker, or similar role and one year facilitating the professional growth of at least one other adult

Option 2:

For those with an Associate degree, four years in a child care setting serving children from birth to 5 years of age, to include:

- Two years working directly with children as a caregiver, teacher, child life worker, social worker, or similar role and two years facilitating the professional growth of at least one other adult

Note: Any early care and learning professionals who only partially meet the eligibility requirements, may still apply to become a CDA Professional Development (PD) Specialist™. A space is provided on the online PD Specialist application, in which interested parties will have the opportunity to provide further explanations. Final determinations of eligibility will be made by the Council.

The CDA Verification Visit® Reflective Dialogue

The CDA 2.0 Verification Visit concludes with a 45-50 minute Reflective Dialogue between Candidate and CDA Professional Development (PD) Specialist™. The purpose of the Dialogue is to support the Candidate's growing skills of professional reflection and goal-setting. The agenda of the Dialogue is as follows:

Welcome, Clarifications (up to 10 min.)

Welcome

- The PD Specialist begins by welcoming the Candidate and reviewing the agenda, expectations and goals for the session by saying "We will be spending 45-50 minutes together. My role is to assist you as you reflect on your continuing professional growth and set new goals for yourself."

Clarifications (optional)

- The PD Specialist uses this time to ask questions regarding any Items in the Comprehensive Scoring Instrument that may still need clarification after the Review and Observation. (i.e., "I wasn't able to read or observe anything about Nap Time. How do you make sure that it is 'a pleasant rest time for all children'?" or "I wasn't able to read or observe anything about how you facilitate meal times. Tell me about how you 'facilitate appropriate mealtime experiences'.")

Reflective Dialogue Introduction, Professional Philosophy Statement (10 min.)

Reflective Dialogue Introduction

- The PD Specialist introduces the Reflective Dialogue by explaining that:

    a. The reflective dialogue will not be scored.

    b. There are no "right" or "wrong" answers in the discussion we're about to have.

- The PD Specialist asks the Candidate to turn to the Reflective Dialogue Worksheet found on p. 141 in this book. During the Reflective Dialogue, she/he will use the Worksheet to record important points to remember about her/his Areas of Professional Strength and Areas for Future Professional Growth. She will then refer to her Worksheet, at the end of the Dialogue, as she/he sets goals and records possible steps to reach each goal.

Professional Philosophy Statement

- The PD Specialist and Candidate discuss the Candidate's Professional Philosophy Statement.

- The PD Specialist asks, "In what ways does your teaching practice reflect your professional philosophy?" or "That's really powerful. How do you make your philosophy come alive?"

Candidate Self-Reflection (10 min.)

Areas of Professional Strength

    a. PD Specialist: "What do you think/believe are your greatest areas of strength as an early childhood professional?"

    b. "Why? How did you develop these areas of strengths?"

    c. "How do you think your areas of strength may positively impact the children and families in your care?"

Areas for Future Professional Growth

    a. PD Specialist: "What do you think/believe are your greatest areas for future growth as an early childhood professional?"

    b. "Why do you think this area(s) is more challenging for you than the areas you mentioned as strengths?"

    c. "How do you think working on these areas for growth may positively impact the children and families in your care?"

PD Specialist Feedback (less than 10 min.)

One Area of Professional Strength

    a. PD Specialist: "Having reviewed your Portfolio and observed you working with children, here is the greatest area of professional strength I documented."

    b. "How did you develop this strength?"

    c. "How do you think this strength may positively impact the children and families in your care?"

One Area for Future Professional Growth

    a. "Here is an area for future professional growth that I documented."

    b. "How might growing in this area positively impact the children and families in your care?"

Goal-Setting & Action-Planning, Close (10 min.)

Goal-Setting

- PD Specialist: "Using the areas of strength and future growth that you've identified and written down on your Reflective Dialogue Worksheet, let's take some time to identify 1 – 3 professional development goals you might set for yourself." (Note: final goals are determined by the Candidate, never by the PD Specialist)

Action-Planning

- PD Specialist: "How will you achieve these goals and by when? Let's brainstorm some actions you might take and timelines for completion. Then you can write them in the appropriate spaces on your Worksheet."

- Candidate and PD Specialist both sign statements at bottom of Worksheet. (The Candidate commits to pursuing goals, the PD Specialist signs to witness the Candidate's commitment)

Close

- PD Specialist: "Thank you for spending this time in the Reflective Dialogue with me. I hope you found it valuable. The Council would like to encourage you to share your goals with a mentor or your supervisor – someone who might hold you accountable and support you in successfully achieving them as you continue to grow as an early childhood professional."

CDA® Exam Questions

The following examples are provided as support for Candidates to understand the nature and structure of the questions they will encounter when they take the Exam. None of the example questions, below, are included in the actual CDA Exam Candidates will take.

As you may notice, the CDA Exam has been carefully designed by national experts to focus on "real life" examples that illustrate a Candidate's ability to put early childhood theory, research and knowledge into practice with young children.

Functional Area: Healthy

Which type of personal item is the healthiest for children to share during choice activities?

    A. Hats

    B. Combs

    C. Play jewelry

    D. Swimming suits

Answer: C. Of the four choices, play jewelry is least likely to transmit infectious materials from child to child. Hats, combs and swimming wear all make contact with sensitive or intimate body areas.

Functional Area: Learning Environment

Of the following, which situation provides the best reason to take children outside to play?

    A. They have been inside for a while, and the weather permits outside play.

    B. They will soon be napping and need to tire themselves out beforehand.

    C. There are fewer adult staff than usual to monitor the indoor activities.

    D. They have become noisy indoors and are not listening to instructions.

Answer: A. Alternating indoor and outdoor play supports children's physical, mental and emotional well-being. The decision to go outdoors should not be made for the reasons given in B, C, and D.

Functional Area: Cognitive

Ms. Lake is planning new activities for four-year-old Hannah. Which consideration is the most important?

    A. What Hannah already knows and can do

    B. What other children in the setting know and can do

    C. What Ms. Lake has succeeded well at teaching

    D. What Hannah will need to know for kindergarten

Answer: A. A is the only choice that focuses directly on Hannah's own learning and development. A, therefore, is a far more important consideration than B, C, and D.

Functional Area: Self

Three-year-old Ayesha is terrified of dogs. Which action is the best first step in helping her overcome her fear?

    A. Approaching her with a gentle dog and asking her to pat its head

    B. Reading stories to her about children who enjoy dogs

    C. Assuring her that there is nothing about dogs to be afraid of

    D. Having a visitor bring in a dog that responds to commands

Answer: B. Stories offer a chance for Ayesha to identify with a character for whom a dog is a friendly companion. Presenting her with a dog at the height of her fears might have an opposite effect to that intended. Telling her that she should not be afraid will not be helpful as a three-year-old does learns best actively rather than by being told.

Functional Area: Guidance

Which means of resolving conflicts is the most beneficial for preschoolers?

    A. Determining which child is at fault so that punishment can be fair

    B. Giving a time-out to each child until each settles down

    C. Helping the children talk and think about solutions to their problems

    D. Using a stern manner and voice to assert control over the situation

Answer: C. The interactions described in C promote children's awareness of their own behavior and the effect of their behavior on others. A, B, and D describe types of punishment and the use of intimidation.

Functional Area: Professionalism

A caregiver would NOT be exhibiting professional behavior by engaging in which of the following activities with a child's family members?

    A. Asking a parent or other family to donate to a favored charity

    B. Discussing childcare issues with the family to help resolve a conflict

    C. Inviting a visiting parent or guardian to eat with the children

    D. Referring a family member to a nonprofit legal-services agency

Answer: A. In general, requesting money from parents for a teacher's personal interests is not consistent with professional behavior. B, C, and D describe actions that are either desirable or neutral.

Glossary of Terms

The following glossary has been arranged in the general order of the CDA Credentialing Process and of this Competency Standards book; the order in which a Candidate might encounter each term.

General

Bilingual Program

A Bilingual program is one which has specific goals for achieving bilingual development in children, in which two languages are consistently used in daily activities and in which families are helped to understand the goals and to support children's bilingual development.

Candidate

An individual who has applied for and has met all eligibility requirements for the CDA Credential.

CDA®

The Child Development Associate® Credential.

Competence/Competency

Skill or ability to do something well.

Competency Standards

Criteria that define the skills that a competent early care and learning professional should demonstrate in working with young children. There are six CDA Competency Standards, 13 Functional Areas, as well as Items, Indicators and Examples that provide further illustrations of the concepts presented. The six Competency Standards are:

I. To establish and maintain a safe, healthy learning environment

II. To advance physical and intellectual competence

III. To support social and emotional development and to provide positive guidance

IV. To establish positive and productive relationships with families

V. To ensure a well-run, purposeful program responsive to participant needs

VI. To maintain a commitment to professionalism

The term Competency Standards is also often used as a shortened name for this book.

Developmental Context

The CDA Competency Standards include a Developmental Context for each of the 13 Functional Areas. It includes a brief summary of children's development and a context for a caregiver's work with children at different stages of development.

Dual Language Learners

Children who are learning two languages simultaneously or adding a new (second) language to their primary (home) language.

Functional Area

A category of responsibility that defines a caregiver's role in relation to children. The six CDA Competency Standards are sorted into the thirteen Functional Areas: Safe, Healthy, Learning Environment, Physical, Cognitive, Communication, Creative, Self, Social, Guidance, Families, Program Management, and Professionalism.

Language Specialization

Candidates may choose to add Specializations to their CDA Credential

- Bilingual Specialization (for Candidates working in bilingual programs)

- Monolingual Specialization (for Candidates working in programs in which a language other than English is spoken)

① Prepare

Clock Hour

60 minutes. Used to determine the 120 required hours of professional education.

Family Questionnaires

The Candidate distributes a Family Questionnaire to each family that has a child in her/his group. The questionnaires give families an opportunity to describe/evaluate the Candidate's work from their point of view and give feedback to the Candidate.

Professional Education

Child care training/preparation for work with children and families. A Candidate must have completed 120 clock hours of such preparation. The CDA Candidate must have had comprehensive instruction in early childhood education/child development in the eight CDA Subject Areas.

Professional Portfolio

The collection of documentation of the Candidate's ability to meet all CDA eligibility requirements. The Portfolio also provides the compilation of the Candidate's reflections on how her/his practice meets the CDA Competency Standards. The Portfolio consists of:

- Transcripts/certificates/letters; documentation of the Candidate's professional education

- Family Questionnaires

- Six Reflective Statements of Competence

- The Resource Collection

- The Professional Philosophy Statement

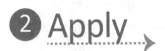 Apply

Application

The online form that you will use to notify the Council that you are ready for your assessment (the CDA Verification Visit® and the CDA Exam). If you are unable to use the online application, you may use the paper version found at the back of this book on p. 129.

Candidate ID Number (#)

The number assigned to you by the Council for Professional Recognition. The number appears in your Confirmation Note and on the printout you receive at the test center confirming that you completed the CDA Exam.

CDA Professional Development (PD) Specialist™

The early childhood education professional, trained and endorsed by the Council to conduct your CDA Verification Visit®.

Conflict of Interest

A relationship that may interfere with a CDA Professional Development (PD) Specialist's™ ability to be objective in assessing a Candidate. Relationships with Candidates that are unacceptable for serving in the PD Specialist role:

- Immediate relative (mother, father, sibling, spouse, son, daughter)

- Current direct supervisor

- Co-worker in same group/classroom

Ready to Schedule Notice

The email or paper notice you will receive from the Council after your CDA application and assessment fee have been successfully processed. The notice allows you to schedule the CDA Exam and gives you the deadline to complete the CDA Exam.

❸ Demonstrate

The CDA® Exam

Confirmation Note

The letter or email you receive from PearsonVUE that confirms your CDA Exam appointment.

Flag

If you are not sure of your answer to an exam question, you may "flag it" for later review by clicking the "flag" button on the computer screen. At the end, if time permits, you will have a chance to review the questions you flagged.

My Account

The account you will create through the PearsonVUE website through which you will schedule and keep track of your CDA Exam.

Nondisclosure Agreement

The required statement seen at the start of the CDA Exam in which you confirm that you are taking the exam because you wish to earn the CDA Credential.

Password

The secret word known only to you that you will use along with your username to enter My Account on the PearsonVUE website to schedule your CDA Exam.

PearsonVUE

Owner and provider of the test centers where you will take the CDA Exam.

Review Screen

The computer screen that will be presented to you after you click through all 65 CDA Exam questions. The screen will show you which questions you have answered (complete), which you have not answered (incomplete) and which questions you flagged for a later review. You may then choose to go back to the various exam questions, if time permits.

Rules Agreement

Agreement that outlines the rules you must follow at the test center. You will be asked to sign the Agreement before entering the testing room.

Username

The unique name you will create, along with your password, that you will use to enter My Account on the PearsonVUE website to schedule your CDA Exam.

Valid Photo ID

The form of identification you must present at the test center in order to take the CDA Exam. Any identification that has not expired and includes your photo will be acceptable. Please note: the name on the ID must match exactly the name you entered on your application.

The CDA Verification Visit®

Comprehensive Scoring Instrument (CSI)

The official form used by the CDA Professional Development (PD) Specialist™ to ascertain and record the Recommended Scores of the Candidate in the 13 Functional Areas using the Candidate's Professional Portfolio and a direct observation of her/him working with children.

Recommended Scores

The Item-level scores determined by the CDA Professional Development (PD) Specialist™ using the Comprehensive Scoring Instrument. The PD Specialist will submit Recommended Scores online to the Council upon completion of the CDA Verification Visit®. These scores are considered "recommended" as they reflect the recommendation of the PD Specialist but do not, in any way, fully determine whether a CDA Credential will be awarded. The CDA Verification Visit Recommended Scores must be combined with the CDA Exam score in order to reach the Cumulative Score the Council will use to determine if the CDA Credential has been earned/awarded.

Reflective Dialogue

The conversation between the Candidate and PD Specialist at the conclusion of the CDA Verification Visit® in which the Candidate reflects on her/his areas of strength and areas for professional growth for the purpose of setting professional goals. The Reflective Dialogue is not scored and therefore has no bearing on the award of the CDA Credential.

The R.O.R. Model®

"R.O.R." stands for Review-Observe-Reflect®, the model used to structure the tasks undertaken by the CDA Professional Development (PD) Specialist™ during the CDA Verification Visit® that contribute to the assessment of Candidate competency. The PD Specialist will Review the Candidate's Professional Portfolio, Observe the Candidate working with children and Reflect with the Candidate on her/his professional strengths and opportunities for growth.

Credential

The written document from the Council for Professional Recognition that verifies that an early care and learning professional has met the CDA Competency Standards.

Renewal

The process of revalidating a CDA Credential when it expires. The CDA Credential is valid for three years from the date of award or renewal. You may apply for renewal of the Credential 90 days before it expires.

APPLY FOR YOUR CDA® ONLINE!

Use *YourCouncil*, the Council's online application, to speed up your credentialing process!

3 things you should know:

1. All CDA credential settings are eligible to apply online.

2. Requests for *Assessments in Other Languages* and *Special Accommodations* can be submitted online.

3. You save $75 by applying online.

With YourCouncil online you can...

- Fill out your application
- Check your status anytime
- Allow your Director to submit statements electronically
- Pay the $425 assessment fee
- Communicate with the Council
- Get automatic updates as to where you are in the credentialing process

APPLY ONLINE TODAY!
yourcouncil.org

COUNCIL
for
PROFESSIONAL
RECOGNITION

CDA
Child Development Associate®
National Credentialing Program

The Child Development Associate® (CDA) Credential™ Application

Please print legibly and be sure to retain a photocopy for your records. Your application processing time will increase significantly if your application is not legible. APPLICATIONS THAT ARE INCOMPLETE OR MISSING PAYMENT WILL BE RETURNED.

A. Candidate Information

Enter your name as it appears on your government issued ID. If your name does not match, you may incur additional fees.

First Name*:

Middle Name:

Last Name*:

Mailing Address*:

Address Continued:

City*:

State*:

Zip Code*:

Email:

Primary Phone #*:

Alternate Phone #:

Date of Birth*:

Month   Date   Year

* Indicates required field

B. Credential Type

Setting (check only one):

☐ Infant/Toddler
(Birth to 36 months)

☐ Preschool
(3 to 5 years)

☐ Family Child Care
(Birth to 5 years)

Language Specialization (optional):

☐ Monolingual Spanish
☐ Bilingual (English and Spanish - see p. 33)
☐ Other monolingual (please indicate other language) _____
☐ Other bilingual, English and (please indicate other language) _____

The Type of Program I am currently working in:

☐ Private Child Care   ☐ Head Start
☐ High School Vocational Program   ☐ Family Child Care
☐ Military Installation _____
☐ Other _____

C. CDA Exam

I will the take the CDA Exam in the following language (check only one):

☐ English ☐ Spanish

Special Accommodations (optional):

I require special accommodations for my CDA Exam. My special accommodations request has been reviewed and approved by the Council and I have attached the signed approval form given to me by the Council. Please see p. 108 for further details.

☐ No

☐ Yes   *If yes: please attach a written explanation and the required official documentation to this application.*

D. Payment

Application Fee: $500.00

Please note that the Application fee is non-refundable and non-transferable. Applications sent without payment will not be processed. Only check, money order or credit card payments will be accepted. Cash will not be accepted.

☐ Enclosed is a non-refundable check or money order made payable to the Council for Professional Recognition.

☐ An agency is paying all or part of my application fee. I have enclosed my payment authorization letter as a substitution for my payment.

☐ I would like to pay with a credit card. ☐ VISA ☐ MASTERCARD ☐ DISCOVER

Card Number: ☐☐☐☐ ☐☐☐☐ ☐☐☐☐ ☐☐☐☐   Dollar Amount: $_____

EXP Date: ☐☐☐   CVC Code: ☐☐☐
Month Year   (3-digit number from back of card)

Name on Card: _____

Billing Address: _____

City: _____ State: _____ Zip Code: _____

Authorized Signature: _____

E. Education

Note that proof of your education will be verified by your CDA Professional Development (PD) Specialist™ during your CDA Verification Visit®. You will need to show valid transcripts, letters or certificates documenting completion of your education.

Please check that you have completed at least ten hours of education in each of the following eight subject areas.

I certify that I have completed a minimum of 10 hours of education related to:

☐ Planning a safe and healthy learning environment.

☐ Advancing children's physical and intellectual development.

☐ Supporting children's social and emotional development.

☐ Building productive relationships with families.

☐ Managing an effective program.

☐ Maintaining a commitment to professionalism.

☐ Observing and recording children's behavior.

☐ Understanding principles of child development and learning.

Total education hours:

☐ I certify that I have completed at least 120 total clock hours of professional ECE education.

Required:

☐ All of my education meets Council requirements as outlined on pp. 10-11.

☐ None of my eligible education was obtained at conferences or from individual consultants.

☐ I have included transcripts, certificates or official letters documenting my education in my Professional Portfolio. I understand that my PD Specialist will review them during my CDA Verification Visit.

F. Eligibility Requirements

☐ I have a minimum of high school diploma / GED or I am enrolled in a high school career/ technical program in early childhood education/child development.

☐ I am able to speak, read and write in the language of my assessment well enough to fulfill the responsibilities of a CDA-credentialed professional.

☐ I have my current certificate of completion or card from a) any first aid course and b) an infant/child (pediatric) CPR course.

☐ I have distributed and collected my Family Questionnaires within the past six months.

☐ The Number of Family Questionnaires distributed and collected: _____

☐ I have 480 hours of experience within the past three (3) years working with children in the same age group and setting for which I am applying.

☐ I have completed my Professional Portfolio within the last six months and according to Council requirements.

   My Professional Portfolio, includes:

   ☐ Majority of Family Questionnaires distributed were collected

   ☐ Six Reflective Competency Statements were written

   ☐ Portfolio includes all of the required Resource Collection items

   ☐ One Professional Philosophy Statement was written

   ☐ *For Infant/Toddler Candidates only:* met all additional requirements

☐ I understand that individuals convicted of a crime involving child abuse or neglect are ineligible to apply for or hold the CDA Credential. If I am awarded the CDA Credential, I agree to meet the standards of the CDA to the best of my ability. I also agree to conduct myself in a professional manner and abide by the *NAEYC Code of Ethical Conduct*. I testify that all answers given to all questions on this application are true to the best of my knowledge.

Candidate Signature:_____   Date: _____

G. My CDA Professional Development (PD) Specialist™

In order to complete the CDA credentialing process, Candidates must participate in a CDA Verification Visit during which their Professional Portfolios will be reviewed, they will be observed working with children and they will participate in a reflective dialogue with a PD Specialist. Applications will only be accepted that include a confirmed PD Specialist for each Candidate (please see p. 20 for information on finding your PD Specialist). Once you contact your PD Specialist and confirm their willingness and availability to serve in this role, ask them to provide you with their full name and PD Specialist identification number:

Full Name of PD Specialist: _____

PD Specialist ID #: _____

NOTE: For those applying for a bilingual or monolingual credential, you must also confirm that the PD Specialist listed above is proficient in the language(s) to be used in the CDA Verification Visit.

☐ I hereby confirm that I have been in direct contact with the person listed above and that she/he has agreed to serve as my PD Specialist. If I have checked this box falsely I am aware that I may be ineligible to receive the CDA Credential and my application fee will not be refunded.

H. Optional Demographic Data

Individual data provided below is optional and will not be shared. The aggregate data will be used for the Council's research purposes only. Your name will remain confidential.

Gender: ☐ Male ☐ Female

Race/Ethnicity:

☐ African American ☐ Asian

☐ Hispanic ☐ Native American

☐ White ☐ Other: _____

Primary Language: _____

Second Language (if applicable): _____

Highest level of education achieved:

☐ High School ☐ Two year college

☐ Four year college ☐ Graduate degree

CDA professional /in-service education (check all that apply):

☐ Four-year college ☐ Two-year college

☐ Career/Technical school ☐ Head Start

☐ Early childhood agency (non Head Start)

☐ Other: _____

If working with children, current title:

☐ Education supervisor / coordinator / specialist

☐ Assistant teacher / Aide ☐ Classroom teacher

☐ Program/Center Director ☐ Home Visitor

☐ Family Child Care Provider ☐ Student

☐ Other: _____

I. Director's Permission Statement (to be filled out by Director, please print legibly)

Full Name: _____

Email address: _____

Center or Family Child Care Program

Center/Program Name: _____

Center/Program Phone #: _____ Director Phone #: _____

Is your center or program licensed or meet state requirements?
☐ Yes ☐ No

If no, is the center or program exempt from licensing?
☐ Yes ☐ No

NOTE: *CDA Verification Visits cannot take place at centers that are not licensed or meet state requirements.*

Director Statement

I understand that a CDA Professional Development (PD) Specialist will conduct a CDA Verification Visit at my center/in my program. The CDA Verification Visit will include a review of the Candidate's portfolio, a classroom observation, and a reflective dialogue.

☐ I agree to find a quiet space for the PD Specialist to spend one hour reviewing the Candidate's portfolio, should the PD Specialist request this space.

☐ I understand that the observation will last for two hours and must take place while the Candidate is actively leading children's activities.

☐ If the Candidate needs to participate in the required reflective dialogue during the work day, I understand that I will need to provide a private space and 45-50 minutes of time during which the Candidate will be away from her/his group of children.

I verify that I am the Director or Family Child Care Provider identified or named in this form. All information I have provided here is accurate. I commit to respect the confidentiality of the Candidate as she/he moves through the CDA credentialing process.

Signature: _____ Date: _____

MY CDA® Professional Portfolio

_____   _____
Candidate Name   Candidate ID Number

Use the following checklist to organize your Professional Portfolio in the order listed below. You may check off each item in the last column as it is completed. Use this "My CDA® Professional Portfolio" sheet as the cover sheet inside your Portfolio. Please see pp. 12-19 for a detailed explanation.

TAB	REQUIRED PORTFOLIO ITEM		✓
	"My CDA Professional Portfolio" cover sheet (this document)		
A	**"Summary of My CDA Education"** cover sheet followed by all relevant training transcripts, certificates and official documentation		
B	**"Family Questionnaires"** cover sheet followed by all completed, returned Family Questionnaires		
C	**"Reflective Dialogue Worksheet"**, completed boxes A and B		
D	**Resource Collection Items**	RC I-1, RC I-2, RC I-3	
	Competency Statement I	CS I, including paragraphs CS I a, CS I b, CS I c	
E	**Resource Collection Items**	RC II-1 through RC II-9	
	Competency Statement II	CS II, including paragraphs CS II a, CS II b, CS II c, CS II d	
F	**Resource Collection Item**	RC III	
	Competency Statement III	CS III, including paragraphs CS III a, CS III b	
G	**Resource Collection Items**	RC IV-1 through RC IV-4	
	Competency Statement IV	CS IV, including paragraphs CS IV a, CS IV b, CS IV c	
H	**Resource Collection Item**	RC V	
	Competency Statement V	CS V, including paragraph CS V a	
I	**Resource Collection Items**	RC VI-1, RC VI-2, RC VI-3	
	Competency Statement VI	CS VI, including paragraphs CS VI a, CS VI b	
J	**Professional Philosophy Statement**		

I attest that the following Professional Portfolio includes Resource Collection items that I gathered, myself, as well as original Statements written by me that reflect my work with the children and families in my care.

_____   _____
Candidate Signature   Date

Summary of My CDA® Education

_____

Candidate Name

Note to Candidate: Please use this summary document as the cover sheet to your "education documentation"; the collection of transcripts, letters, certificates, etc. that you will place in your Professional Portfolio to document how you met the educational requirements for the CDA® Credential. At your CDA Verification Visit®, your CDA Professional Development (PD) Specialist™ will review this sheet to ensure that it accurately reflects your education documentation that follows. Please see p. 11 for a detailed explanation of acceptable professional education.

Statements of CDA® Education Completion:

I attest to completing the required 10 hours of education in each of the following CDA Subject Areas.

CDA® Subject Areas	Please initial below
1. Planning a safe, healthy learning environment	
2. Advancing children's physical and intellectual development	
3. Supporting children's social and emotional development	
4. Building productive relationships with families	
5. Managing an effective program	
6. Maintaining a commitment to professionalism	
7. Observing and recording children's behavior	
8. Understanding principles of child development and learning	

I attest to the accuracy of the above Statements of Completion: that I completed at least 10 clock hours of professional education in each of the 8 CDA Subject Areas. I also attest that I have met or exceeded 120 total clock hours of CDA-related professional education.

_____   _____
Candidate Signature   Date

Family Questionnaire

Introduction

_____ is preparing to earn the nationally-renowned Child Development Associate® (CDA) Credential™. In order to be awarded the CDA®, she/he has taken on a significant professional challenge: She/he must have experience working with young children, must have a required amount of early childhood education, must prepare a Professional Portfolio, must be observed working by a skilled professional (a CDA Professional Development (PD) Specialist™) and must pass the national CDA Exam.

The process of getting a CDA is also a professional development experience in which Candidates reflect on areas of strength and areas for future professional growth. In addition to self-reflection, Candidates are provided feedback to consider by the CDA Professional Development (PD) Specialist™ and by you, if you so choose. So, we invite you to complete the questionnaire, below, in order to provide feedback that may help the Candidate continue to grow as a professional.

Please know that:

    a) Completing this questionnaire is optional. If you choose to complete it, your feedback will only be read by the Candidate in order to contribute important information that may assist her/him in setting professional goals for the coming year. **The answers you provide on this questionnaire will have no impact on whether the Candidate will be awarded the CDA Credential.**

    b) You may provide your feedback anonymously, if you so choose.

If you choose to complete the questionnaire, you must return it to the Candidate by _____.

Family Questionnaire

Each of the following topics relates to key areas of quality early childhood professional practice as outlined by the Council for Professional Recognition. For each area, please rate the Candidate on a scale of 1 – 3 in which 1 = Needs improvement/Area for professional growth, 2 = Capable/Competent and 3 = Very capable/Area of strength.

    The Candidate:

       1. Provides a safe, clean environment for my child and teaches her/him how to stay safe | 1 | 2 | 3 |

       2. Provides an environment that promotes health and good nutrition | 1 | 2 | 3 |

3. Provides activities, materials and schedules that promote my child's development and education

1	2	3

4. Uses activities, materials and equipment that allow my child to develop small muscle skills (like writing or pouring) and large muscle skills (like climbing or balancing)

1	2	3

5. Uses activities, materials and equipment that help my child learn how to think, reason and solve problems

1	2	3

6. Helps my child learn how to communicate and introduces her/him to the basics of reading and writing

1	2	3

7. Helps my child express herself/himself creatively through music, art and movement

1	2	3

8. Nurtures my child, helping her/him build a positive self-identity and respect for every child's cultural backgrounds

1	2	3

9. Helps my child learn how to socialize and get along with others

1	2	3

10. Uses effective strategies to help my child understand how to behave appropriately

1	2	3

11. Establishes positive, responsive and cooperative relationships with myself and the members of our family

1	2	3

12. Is well-organized and effectively manages the classroom or group

1	2	3

13. Presents herself/himself in a professional manner

1	2	3

14. (for Bilingual Specialization Candidates only) Respectfully communicates with my family in our preferred language

1	2	3

_____

Name (optional)

Thank you for taking the time to support the Candidate's professional growth. If you would like to provide additional feedback, please feel free to attach it to this questionnaire.

COUNCIL
— for —
PROFESSIONAL
RECOGNITION

Cuestionario para la Familia

Introducción

_____ se está preparando para obtener la nacionalmente reconocida credencial de Asociado en Desarrollo Infantil (CDA®). Con el fin de recibir esta credencial CDA, él/ella ha tomado un desafío profesional significativo: Él/ella debe tener experiencia trabajando con niños pequeños, debe tener una cantidad de cursos requeridos de educación infantil, debe preparar un Portafolio Profesional, debe ser observado(a) por un profesional calificado (un Especialista CDA en Desarrollo Profesional) mientras trabaja con niños y debe aprobar el Examen CDA.

El proceso para obtener la credencial CDA también es una experiencia de desarrollo profesional en la que el Candidato reflexiona sobre sus áreas de fortaleza y sus áreas para un futuro desarrollo profesional. Además de la auto-reflexión, a los Candidatos se les brinda comentarios sobre su desempeño que deben considerar. Estos comentarios los ofrece el Especialista CDA en Desarrollo Profesional y usted, si usted decide colaborar. Por ello, le invitamos a completar el cuestionario que se encuentra abajo, con el fin de brindar comentarios que puedan ayudar al Candidato a continuar su desarrollo como profesional.

Por favor, sepa que:

a) Completar este cuestionario es opcional. Si usted decide completarlo, sus comentarios solo serán leídos por el Candidato con el fin de proporcionar información importante que pueda ayudarlo(a) a establecer sus metas profesionales para el próximo año. **Las respuestas que usted brinde en este cuestionario no tendrán impacto en la decisión de otorgar o no la credencial CDA al Candidato.**

b) Usted puede brindar sus comentarios de manera anónima, si lo desea.

Si usted elige completar el cuestionario, debe devolverlo al Candidato antes del _____.

Cuestionario para la Familia

Cada uno de los siguientes temas se relaciona a las áreas claves de prácticas profesionales de calidad en educación infantil indicadas por el Concilio para el Reconocimiento Profesional. Para cada área, por favor califique al Candidato en una escala de 1 – 3 en la cual: 1 = Necesita mejorar/Área para el desarrollo profesional, 2 = Capaz/Competente y 3 = Muy capaz/Área de fortaleza.

El Candidato:

1. Brinda un ambiente seguro y limpio para mi hijo y le enseña cómo permanecer seguro.

| 1 | 2 | 3 |

2. Brinda un ambiente que fomenta la salud y la buena nutrición.

| 1 | 2 | 3 |

3. Brinda actividades, materiales y horarios que fomentan el desarrollo y la educación de mi hijo.

| 1 | 2 | 3 |

4. Utiliza actividades, materiales y equipo que permiten a mi hijo desarrollar las habilidades de su motricidad fina (como escribir o verter líquidos) y las habilidades de su motricidad gruesa (como trepar o balancearse).

| 1 | 2 | 3 |

5. Utiliza actividades, materiales y equipo que ayudan a mi hijo a aprender cómo pensar, razonar y resolver problemas.

| 1 | 2 | 3 |

6. Ayuda a mi hijo a aprender cómo comunicarse y le presenta los conceptos básicos de lectura y escritura.

| 1 | 2 | 3 |

7. Ayuda a mi hijo a expresarse de manera creativa a través de la música, arte y movimiento.

| 1 | 2 | 3 |

8. Brinda afecto a mi hijo, ayudándolo a edificar una identidad positiva de sí mismo y respetar los orígenes culturales de cada niño.

| 1 | 2 | 3 |

9. Ayuda a mi hijo a aprender a cómo socializar y llevarse bien con otras personas.

| 1 | 2 | 3 |

10. Utiliza estrategias eficaces para ayudar a mi hijo a comprender cómo comportarse de manera apropiada.

| 1 | 2 | 3 |

11. Establece relaciones positivas, receptivas y cooperativas conmigo y los miembros de nuestra familia.

| 1 | 2 | 3 |

12. Es bien organizado y dirige eficazmente el salón de clases o grupo.

| 1 | 2 | 3 |

13. Se comporta de una manera profesional.

| 1 | 2 | 3 |

14. (sólo para Candidatos de Especialización Bilingüe) Se comunica respetuosamente con mi familia en nuestro idioma de preferencia.

| 1 | 2 | 3 |

_____

Nombre (opcional)

Gracias por tomarse tiempo para apoyar el crecimiento profesional del Candidato. Si le gustaría brindar comentarios adicionales, por favor no dude en adjuntarlos a este cuestionario.

COUNCIL
— for —
PROFESSIONAL
RECOGNITION

Family Questionnaires Summary Sheet

_____   _____
Candidate Name   Candidate ID Number

Once you have distributed and collected your Family Questionnaires, place them behind Tab B in your Professional Portfolio. Complete this Summary Sheet and put it in front of the completed questionnaires.

1. I distributed _____ Family Questionnaires.

2. I collected _____ Family Questionnaires and placed them behind this Summary sheet. Therefore, I collected the "majority" (more than half) of the Questionnaires I distributed.

3. I have looked for patterns or trends of feedback from these Questionnaires. Upon reflection, I think some of the families see the following as my greatest professional strength(s) and area(s) for professional growth:

Area(s) of Strength (list at least one)

_____

_____

_____

Area(s) for Professional Growth (list at least one)

_____

_____

_____

4. I have taken the areas of strength and growth that I wrote, above, and entered them into Boxes A and B in my Reflective Dialogue Worksheet at the end of this book.

Note to the CDA PD Specialist™:

Please do not read the contents of the Family Questionnaires found behind this Summary Sheet. This feedback is private, between this Candidate and the families she/he serves. Simply count the Questionnaires and verify that the number of questionnaires behind this Summary sheet matches the number written in #2, above. If the number matches, consider this required task complete. If the number does not match record this information in Item 13.4 of the _Comprehensive Scoring Instrument_.

CDA Verification Visit® Reflective Dialogue Worksheet

Note to Candidate: The last step of the CDA Verification Visit process is the reflective dialogue, the culminating activity designed to support your ongoing reflection about your professional practices. Please know that the dialogue you will have with your CDA Professional Development (PD) Specialist™ will be kept confidential between the two of you, will not be scored and has no bearing on the award of your CDA® Credential. You will retain this worksheet after the dialogue – no one else will see this worksheet unless you choose to share it. Therefore, feel free to reflect honestly and candidly about your professional strengths and areas for growth. There are no "right" or "wrong" answers in a reflective dialogue – only your commitment to your own professional growth and the goals you will set for yourself.

Step 1: Identify Areas of Strength and Areas for Future Professional Growth

In order to identify the best goals for yourself, it may be helpful to first explore different perspectives – (1) opinions from the families you serve, (2) your own thoughts and (3) feedback from your PD Specialist, who has just read your *Professional Portfolio* and observed you working with children. Before your CDA Verification Visit, please read the *Family Questionnaires* you received. Look for trends or patterns of responses and write down, in boxes A and B below, as many areas of strength and areas for professional growth that you would like. You will complete the second and third columns during the reflective dialogue.

	1. Family Questionnaires (to be completed by the candidate prior to the CDA Verification Visit)	2. Candidate Self-Reflection (to be completed by the candidate during the reflective dialogue)	3. Feedback From My PD Specialist (to be completed by the candidate during the reflective dialogue)
What are Your Area(s) of Professional Strength?	A	C	E
What are your Area(s) for Future Professional Growth?	B	D	F

Step 2: Set Goals, Plan Action Steps

Now that you have listed your perceived strengths and areas for future growth, what goal or goals might you set for yourself? Is there a strength you're committed to strengthening even further? Is there an area you've identified that you are committed to improving? In the spaces below, list up to three professional goals you are committed to achieving. After writing each goal, discuss with your PD Specialist steps you might take to reach that goal.

Goal #1:	Steps I could take to reach Goal #1:
Goal #2:	Steps I could take to reach Goal #2:
Goal #3:	Steps I could take to reach Goal #3:

Step 3: Commit to Achieving Your Goal(s)

I, _____, hereby commit to achieving my goal(s) in order to further develop as a professional and to become even more effective at serving the needs of the children and families in my care.

_____   _____
CDA Candidate (sign here)   as witnessed by my CDA PD Specialist (sign here)

This worksheet is now yours to keep. Being a reflective practitioner and meeting the goals you've set for yourself is up to you, regardless of whether you are awarded your CDA Credential. The Council encourages you to share your goals with a mentor, colleague or supervisor who will support you, hold you accountable for meeting your goals and celebrate with you when you have met them.

Comprehensive Scoring Instrument

Candidate's Name: _____

Credential Type: ☐ Infant/Toddler   ☐ Preschool   ☐ Family Child Care

Bilingual Specialization: ☐ Yes   ☐ No

Date of Portfolio Review: _____

Date of Observation: _____

Instructions for the CDA Professional Development (PD) Specialist™:

The CDA Comprehensive Scoring Instrument (CSI) is the tool you will utilize to determine the competencies of the Candidate named above, using multiple sources of evidence:

(1) the contents of the Candidate's Professional Portfolio

(2) your direct observation of the Candidate working with young children and

(3) your skilled perceptions of the care/education environments that the Candidate is responsible for designing/maintaining (when applicable)

Structure of the CSI

The CSI was designed to reflect the nationally-recognized CDA Competency Standards, found on p. 40. in this book, that provide a baseline of competencies for all professionals working with, educating and caring for groups of young children.

In order to best elaborate on the key professional practices identified, the Standards in this tool have been arranged according to the following hierarchy:

Functional Area

Item/Item/Item

Indicator

CDA PD Specialists™ are responsible for using the CSI tool to determine and submit to the Council Recommended Scores (1 – 3) at the Item level. In order to assist you in this endeavor, it is recommended that you review and observe at the Indicator level, later using your professional judgment to assign Item scores based on the averages or patterns you have recorded of that Item's related Indicators.

In order to best determine Indicator scores you may need to consult the various optional examples listed in the Competency Standards section of the book. Please remember that these examples are optional and are provided only for the purposes of illustration. They were not designed to be an inclusive list that every Candidate must display in order to be assigned a Recommended Score.

Please also note that the CSI has been designed as a universal tool that can be used for all CDA Credentials: Preschool, Infant/Toddler and Family Child Care. Indicators must be interpreted using the specific examples listed in the book related to that Credential type (in other words, preschool examples may be different than infant/toddler examples). Additional examples have also been provided and must be taken into consideration for certain Items when reviewing and observing a Candidate applying for Bilingual Specialization.

Leave these CSI pages attached to the book during the CDA Verification Visit® in order to quickly
consult the examples for clarification whenever needed.

Use of the CSI

You will rate the Candidate on a scale of 1 – 3: | 1 | 2 | 3 |

   1 = Little or no evidence

   2 = Some evidence

   3 = Great deal of evidence

Full instructions for use of the CSI can be accessed by PD Specialists in the Professional Development Specialist (PDS) Resource Library. Note: When submitting a score of 1 to the Council online, the PD Specialist will be required to add a brief note explaining the rationale and/or examples for that score.

Sections of the CSI

In order to make your use of the tool as efficient as possible during the Verification Visit, the CSI has been sorted into three color-coded sections:

Settings & Activities

This section includes all of the Items that do not rely on Candidate behaviors. In other words, you will be able to assess these Items without the Candidate present; by reading the related topics in the Candidate's Professional Portfolio and/or by looking at the children's environments (spaces, furniture, equipment, materials, etc.) for which the Candidate is responsible.

NOTE: If the Candidate is not responsible for designing/maintaining the environment(s) in which the Observation occurs, you will need to rely more heavily on the related writings/resources found in her/his Reflective Competency Statement about "Competency Standard I: Safe, Healthy Learning Environments" when reviewing the Portfolio.

Actions & Interactions

This section will be the primary section used during your observation of the Candidate working with children (minimum of two hours). All of the Items in this section relate to Candidate behaviors; the ways you observe she/he acting and interacting with children.

Review

This section includes all of the Items that are typically unobservable. In order to determine Recommended Scores for each of these Items, you will likely need to rely solely on what you read in the Candidate's Professional Portfolio during the one-hour Review session.

Final Steps

The final step, once you have completed the Review and Observe sessions using this CSI, is to facilitate the Reflect Session with the Candidate. During this session, you may ask questions of clarification to assist you in completing the CSI. You will also discuss the Candidate's Professional Philosophy Statement and provide the Candidate with your feedback about one "Area of Professional Strength" and one "Area for Professional Growth" based on your review and observation. To prepare, feel free to use the "Reminders to Myself to Prepare for the Reflective Dialogue" sheet found on the last page of this CSI.

Upon completion of the Verification Visit, you must remove the CSI from this book using the perforations on the inside of each page. You will then return the book to the Candidate and take the CSI with you in order to use when you submit this Candidate's Recommended Scores to the Council through the Submission Tool in the online PD Specialist Portal.

In order to protect Candidate confidentiality, the PD Specialist may not share or make copies of the notes or Recommended Scores recorded on the CSI with/for any person, including the Candidate. Once the Recommended Scores have been submitted to the Council online, the PD Specialist is required to shred or otherwise destroy this CSI tool.

Functional Area 1: SAFE

Item 1.1 Environments are safe for all children and adults. (p. 42)

1	2	3

Indicator:

a) _____ Materials, equipment and environments are safe

Item 1.2 Well-planned and well-organized emergency procedures and supplies are evident. (p. 43)

1	2	3

Indicators:

a) _____ Procedures for fires and other emergencies are posted

b) _____ First-aid supplies and medicines are stored appropriately and accessible to adults only

Optional Notes: SAFE (Items 1.1, 1.2 above)

Review Notes	Observation Notes

Functional Area 2: HEALTHY

Item 2.1 Children's settings promote good health. (p. 46)

1	2	3

Indicators:

a) _____ Materials, equipment and environments are clean and promote good health

b) _____ Disinfecting and sanitizing solutions are present and stored appropriately

c) _____ Relevant health information from families of children are maintained and posted

Optional Notes: HEALTHY (Item 2.1 above)

Review Notes	Observation Notes

Settings & Activities

Functional Area 3: LEARNING ENVIRONMENT

Item 3.1 Environments are developmentally appropriate for young children. (p. 50)

1	2	3

Indicators:

a) _____ Environments are pleasant, welcoming and provide appropriate levels of stimulation

b) _____ Environments are arranged and organized intentionally to meet the developmental needs of children

Item 3.2 Developmentally appropriate materials are available. (p. 52)

1	2	3

Indicators:

a) _____ Materials are developmentally appropriate for all children

b) _____ A variety of materials are provided for children to explore

c) _____ There is a sufficient number of materials to accommodate the group size

d) _____ Materials are organized and accessible to children throughout the day

Item 3.3 Daily schedule and weekly plan(s) are developmentally appropriate. (p. 53)

1	2	3

Indicators:

a) _____ Schedule allows for routine needs of children to be met

b) _____ Schedule provided meets children's needs for play

c) _____ Whole group times, when offered, are developmentally appropriate

d) _____ Weekly Plans provide a variety of developmentally appropriate experiences

e) _____ Pleasant nap or quiet times meet children's needs for rest

Optional Notes: LEARNING ENVIRONMENT (Items 3.1, 3.2, 3.3 above)

Review Notes	Observation Notes

Settings & Activities

Functional Area 4: PHYSICAL

Item 4.1 Activities, materials and equipment encourage children of varying abilities to develop their large muscles. (p. 59)

| 1 | 2 | 3 |

Indicator:

a) _____ Gross motor skills are encouraged through developmentally appropriate materials, equipment and indoor/outdoor activities

Item 4.2 Activities and materials encourage children of varying abilities to develop their small muscles. (p. 60)

| 1 | 2 | 3 |

Indicator:

a) _____ Individual fine motor skills are encouraged through a variety of developmentally appropriate materials and activities

Item 4.3 Activities and materials encourage children to develop their senses. (p. 60)

| 1 | 2 | 3 |

Indicator:

a) _____ Sight, sound, smell, taste, and touch experiences are encouraged through a variety of developmentally appropriate materials and activities

Optional Notes: PHYSICAL (Items 4.1, 4.2, 4.3 above)

Review Notes	Observation Notes

Functional Area 5: COGNITIVE

Item 5.1 Activities encourage curiosity, exploration and discovery. (p. 62)

| 1 | 2 | 3 |

Indicator:

a) _____ Activities involve developmentally appropriate, hands-on experiences

Settings & Activities

Item 5.2 Materials and equipment stimulate children's thinking and problem solving. (p. 63)

1	2	3

Indicators:

a) _____ Materials and equipment provide a variety of opportunities for cognitive development

b) _____ Materials chosen are meaningful to the children

Optional Notes: COGNITIVE (Items 5.1, 5.2 above)

Review Notes	Observation Notes

Functional Area 6: COMMUNICATION

Item 6.1 Materials promote early literacy. (p. 66)

1	2	3

Indicators:

a) _____ Literature/storytelling/bookmaking materials are provided

b) _____ Developmentally appropriate books are available

Item 6.2 Activities promote language development. (p. 67)

1	2	3

Indicators:

a) _____ Children are read to every day

b) _____ Activities advance the development of language acquisition and writing skills

c) _____ Activities provide frequent opportunities for children to listen, talk and express their ideas effectively

d) _____ Activities support the needs of dual language learners (when applicable)

Optional Notes: COMMUNICATION (Items 6.1, 6.2 above)

Review Notes	Observation Notes

Settings & Activities

Functional Area 7: CREATIVE

Item 7.1 Activities and materials encourage children to express themselves through the visual arts. (p. 73)

| 1 | 2 | 3 |

Indicators:

a) _____ Art materials and activities are available for children daily

Item 7.2 Activities and materials encourage children to dance, move and develop their musical abilities. (p. 74)

| 1 | 2 | 3 |

Indicators:

a) _____ Music and dance/movement materials and activities are available for children daily

Item 7.3 Activities and materials provided encourage children to develop their imaginations. (p. 74)

| 1 | 2 | 3 |

Indicators:

a) _____ Dramatic play materials and activities are available for children daily

Optional Notes: CREATIVE (Items 7.1, 7.2, 7.3 above)

Review Notes	Observation Notes

Functional Area 8: SELF

Item 8.1 Children's environments support the development of positive self-concepts. (p. 78)

| 1 | 2 | 3 |

Indicators:

a) _____ Spaces and activities help each child develop a sense of self-identity/worth

b) _____ Materials chosen provide children opportunities to experience success

Settings & Activities

Optional Notes: SELF (Item 8.1 above)

Review Notes	Observation Notes

Functional Area 9: SOCIAL

Item 9.1 **The classroom environment provides opportunities for children to experience cooperation.** (p. 83)　　1 | **2** | **3**

Indicator:

a) _____ Materials, equipment and activities provided help children experience working and playing in harmony

Item 9.2 **A non-biased environment is provided.** (p. 83)　　1 | **2** | **3**

Indicator:

a) _____ Diverse activities, materials, curricula and/or events reflect multiple cultural groups, ethnicities and family structures

Optional Notes: SOCIAL (Items 9.1, 9.2 above)

Review Notes	Observation Notes

Settings & Activities

Functional Area 10: GUIDANCE

Item 10.1 Spaces and materials are arranged to promote positive interactions and limit disruptive behaviors. (p. 88)

1	2	3

Indicator:

a) _____ Spaces and materials provided anticipate children's behavioral and developmental needs

Optional Notes: GUIDANCE (Item 10.1 above)

Review Notes	Observation Notes

Functional Area 11: FAMILIES

Item 11.1 Various opportunities to appreciate and communicate with children's families are included as part of the regular program. (p. 94)

1	2	3

Indicators:

a) _____ Room displays and materials reflect respect for various communities, cultural groups and families

b) _____ Opportunities to communicate with and distribute information to families are provided

Optional Notes: FAMILIES (Item 11.1 above)

Review Notes	Observation Notes

Settings & Activities

Functional Area 1: SAFE

Item 1.3 Candidate ensures children's safety at all times. (p. 43)

1	2	3

Indicators:

a) _____ Ensures that children are attended by authorized adults at all times

b) _____ Teaches children appropriate safety practices

c) _____ Provides attentive supervision at all times

d) _____ Makes sure that foods that are known choking hazards are not served

Optional Notes: SAFE (Item 1.3 above)

Review Notes	Observation Notes

Functional Area 2: HEALTHY

Item 2.2 Candidate implements appropriate hygiene practices to minimize the spread of infectious diseases. (p. 46)

1	2	3

Indicators:

a) _____ Cleans/sanitizes materials and equipment

b) _____ Uses correct hand washing procedures before and after serving food, diapering/toileting and whenever needed

c) _____ Implements sanitary diapering/toileting procedures

Item 2.3 Candidate encourages children to practice healthy habits. (p. 47)

1	2	3

Indicators:

a) _____ Ensures that older children wash hands properly, with assistance when needed

b) _____ Models, communicates and provides activities that teach the importance of good health to children and families

Actions & Interactions

Item 2.4 Candidate provides appropriate mealtime experiences.

(p. 49)

| 1 | 2 | 3 |

Indicators:

a) _____ Serves nutritious meals and snacks

b) _____ Facilitates appropriate mealtime experiences

Optional Notes: HEALTHY (Items 2.3, 2.4, 2.5 above)

Review Notes	Observation Notes

Functional Area 3: LEARNING ENVIRONMENT

Item 3.4 Candidate's disposition is warm and welcoming. (p. 55)

| 1 | 2 | 3 |

Indicator:

a) _____ Creates a nurturing relationship with each child

Item 3.5 Candidate demonstrates sound judgment in using the posted Weekly Schedule/Daily Plan. (p. 56)

| 1 | 2 | 3 |

Indicators:

a) _____ Generally follows posted schedule and plan

b) _____ Veers from schedule and plan as needed

Item 3.6 Uses a variety of strategies to transition children from one activity to another. (p. 57)

| 1 | 2 | 3 |

Indicator:

a) _____ Demonstrates an understanding of the importance of transitions

Optional Notes: LEARNING ENVIRONMENT (Items 3.4, 3.5, 3.6 above)

Review Notes	Observation Notes

Actions & Interactions

Functional Area 4: PHYSICAL

Item 4.4 Candidate's facilitation promotes children's physical development. (p. 61)

1	2	3

Indicators:

a) _____ Participates in physical activities with children, when appropriate

b) _____ Guides the development of children's fine and gross motor skills

Optional Notes: PHYSICAL (Item 4.4 above)

Review Notes	Observation Notes

Functional Area 5: COGNITIVE

Item 5.3 Candidate's interactions promote children's thinking and problem solving. (p. 64)

1	2	3

Indicators:

a) _____ Facilitates children's thinking and creative problem-solving skills

Item 5.4 Candidate's interactions intentionally build upon children's previous knowledge. (p. 65)

1	2	3

Indicators:

a) _____ Connects concepts to children's prior experiences

b) _____ Supports children's repetition of the familiar

Optional Notes: COGNITIVE (Items 5.3, 5.4 above)

Review Notes	Observation Notes

Actions & Interactions

Functional Area 6: COMMUNICATION

Item 6.3 Candidate reads to children in a developmentally appropriate manner. (p. 69)

| 1 | 2 | 3 |

Indicators:

a) _____ Reads to children engagingly

Item 6.4 Candidate's interactions encourage children's communication skills. (p. 70)

| 1 | 2 | 3 |

Indicators:

a) _____ Promotes children's language development through her/his verbal and non-verbal communications

b) _____ Interacts with children, listening and responding appropriately

c) _____ Supports the needs of dual language learners (when applicable)

Item 6.5 Candidate promotes children's vocabulary development. (p. 71)

| 1 | 2 | 3 |

Indicators:

a) _____ Intentionally provides opportunities for children to learn new words.

b) _____ Regularly introduces children to more advanced vocabulary

Optional Notes: COMMUNICATION (Items 6.3, 6.4, 6.5 above)

Review Notes	Observation Notes

Functional Area 7: CREATIVE

Item 7.4 Candidate promotes individual expression and creativity. (p. 75)

| 1 | 2 | 3 |

Indicators:

a) _____ Encourages creative self-expression in children's activities

b) _____ Facilitates child-directed and process-oriented creative experiences

Actions & Interactions

Optional Notes: CREATIVE (Item 7.4 above)

Review Notes	Observation Notes

Functional Area 8: SELF

Item 8.2 Candidate's interactions help children develop positive self-concepts. (p. 79)

1	2	3

Indicators:

a) _____ Respects the individuality of each child

b) _____ Shows sensitivity to and acceptance of each child's feelings and needs

Item 8.3 Candidate encourages children to develop a sense of independence. (p. 81)

1	2	3

Indicators:

a) _____ Encourages children's self-help/self-regulation skills while being respectful of family preferences and cultural differences

b) _____ Ensures that toileting is a developmentally appropriate, positive experience for children

c) _____ Promotes each child's growing sense of autonomy

Optional Notes: SELF (Items 8.2, 8.3, 8.4 above)

Review Notes	Observation Notes

Actions & Interactions

Functional Area 9: SOCIAL

Item 9.3 Candidate promotes children's sense of belonging in the classroom community. (p. 84)

1	2	3

Indicators:

a) _____ Encourages children's social interactions

b) _____ Models appropriate social interactions

1 = Little or no evidence   2 = Some evidence   3 = Great deal of evidence

Item 9.4 Candidate helps children experience sympathy/empathy and respect for others. (p. 86)

| 1 | 2 | 3 |

Indicators:

a) _____ Helps children understand their feelings and the feelings of others

b) _____ Discusses diversity comfortably when interacting with children

Optional Notes: SOCIAL (Items 9.3, 9.4 above)

Review Notes	Observation Notes

Functional Area 10: GUIDANCE

Item 10.2 Candidate proactively implements methods for preventing behavioral problems. (p. 88)

| 1 | 2 | 3 |

Indicators:

a) _____ Acknowledges positive behaviors

b) _____ Models appropriate behaviors

c) _____ Provides firm, consistent limits and expectations

d) _____ Uses effective classroom management techniques

e) _____ Helps children learn to articulate their emotions and practice how to respond in challenging situations

Item 10.3 Candidate uses positive techniques when reacting to children's challenging behaviors. (p. 91)

| 1 | 2 | 3 |

Indicators:

a) _____ Places emphasis on the development of self-discipline/self-regulation

b) _____ Deals with challenging behavior in a consistent and calm manner

c) _____ Uses appropriate techniques to address negative behaviors

Optional Notes: GUIDANCE (Items 10.2, 10.3 above)

Review Notes	Observation Notes

Actions & Interactions

Note to the CDA Professional Development (PD) Specialist™:

The following Items have been categorized as "Review" Items as they may not be fully observable in a typically-scheduled CDA Verification Visit®. Therefore the Council recommends that you primarily base your Recommended Scores on the Reflective Competency Statements and Resources in the Candidate's Professional Portfolio that you will read during the Review Session.

Functional Area 11: FAMILIES

Item 11.2 Candidate appreciates the uniqueness of each family. (p. 95)

1	2	3

Indicators:

a) _____ Welcomes and respects every family

Item 11.3 Candidate partners with families to support the needs of their children. (p. 96)

1	2	3

Indicators:

a) _____ Works closely with each family

b) _____ Maintains open communication with families

Item 11.4 Candidate helps families understand and support the healthy growth and development of their child. (p. 98)

1	2	3

Indicators:

a) _____ Provides information and opportunities to help families meet their child's developmental needs

b) _____ Knows the social service, health and education resources of the community, engaging them when appropriate

c) _____ Recommends activities families can do at home that support their child's development

Optional Notes: FAMILIES (Items 11.2, 11.3, 11.4 above)

Review Notes	Observation Notes

Functional Area 12: PROGRAM MANAGEMENT

Item 12.1 Candidate observes, documents and assesses each child's developmental/educational progress. (p. 101)

| 1 | 2 | 3 |

Indicators:

a) _____ Objectively observes and records information about children's behaviors and learning

b) _____ Analyzes and assesses multiple sources of evidence in order to set appropriate developmental goals for each child/group, planning curriculum accordingly

Item 12.2 Candidate adheres to regulatory requirements and program policies. (p. 102)

| 1 | 2 | 3 |

Indicators:

a) _____ Adheres to current local child care regulations and program policies

b) _____ Adheres to professional Mandated Reporting requirements related to abuse and neglect

c) _____ Maintains current records on children's health, safety and behavior

Item 12.3 Candidate maintains effective professional relationships. (p. 103)

| 1 | 2 | 3 |

Indicator:

a) _____ Establishes cooperative interpersonal relationships with coworkers, colleagues, volunteers and supervisors

Note: You may find some needed evidence for this Item during the Observe Session, if the Candidate is observed working with another teacher or colleague.

Optional Notes: PROGRAM MANAGEMENT (Items 12.1, 12.2, 12.3 above)

Review Notes	Observation Notes

Functional Area 13: PROFESSIONALISM

Item 13.1 Candidate commits to highest standards for professional practices. (p. 104)

1	2	3

Indicators:

a) _____ Protects the confidentiality of information about children, their families and the child care program

b) _____ Conducts her/himself in a professional manner at all times

Item 13.2 Candidate works with other professionals and families to communicate the needs of children and families to decision makers. (p. 105)

1	2	3

Indicators:

a) _____ Advocates for the needs of children and families

Item 13.3 Candidate takes advantage of opportunities to continue professional growth. (p. 105)

1	2	3

Indicator:

a) _____ Learns about new laws and regulations affecting child care, children, and families

b) _____ Takes opportunities for professional and personal development by reflecting, joining professional organizations and attending meetings, training courses and conferences

(Continued on next page)

1 = Little or no evidence   2 = Some evidence   3 = Great deal of evidence

Review

Note to the CDA Professional Development (PD) Specialist™:

One clear sign of the Candidate's professionalism is her/his completion of the Professional Portfolio as a requirement of the credentialing process. Therefore, the following Item should also receive a Recommended Score:

1	☒	3

Item 13.4 Candidate has completed all requirements of the CDA Professional Portfolio in preparation for this CDA Verification Visit®. (pp. 12-19)

3 = All Portfolio requirements met

1 = One or more Portfolio requirements were not met

(If 1, the PD Specialist is required to add a brief note explaining the rationale and/or examples for that score)

Indicators:

a) _____ Majority of Family Questionnaires distributed were collected

b) _____ Six Reflective Competency Statements were written

c) _____ Portfolio includes all of the required Resource Collection items

d) _____ One Professional Philosophy Statement was written

Optional Notes: PROFESSIONALISM (Items 13.1, 13.2, 13.3, 13.4)

Review Notes	Observation Notes